Historical Commentary on the Pastoral Epistles

Historical Commentary on the Pastoral Epistles

WILLIAM M. RAMSAY

Edited by Mark Wilson

kregel
PUBLICATIONS

Grand Rapids, MI 49501

Historical Commentary on the Pastoral Epistles
by Sir William M. Ramsay

Copyright © 1996 by Kregel Publications, a division of Kregel, Inc., P.O. Box 2607, Grand Rapids, MI 49501. Kregel Publications provides trusted, biblical publications for Christian growth and service. Your comments and suggestions are valued.

Cover design: Alan G. Hartman
Book design: Nicholas G. Richardson
Library of Congress Cataloging-in-Publication Data
Ramsay, William Mitchell, Sir, 1851–1939
    Historical commentary on the pastoral epistles / Sir William M. Ramsay.
        p.   cm.
Previously "published in The Expositor, Seventh series, 7 and 8 (1909); 9 (1910); Eighth series, 1 (1911)"—Introd.
Includes bibliographical references.
    1. Bible. N.T. Pastoral Epistles—Criticism, interpretation, etc. I. Title.
BS2735.2.R35   1996   227'8307—dc20   96-10313
                                                                            CIP
ISBN 0-8254-3636-2

Printed in the United States of America
1 2 3 4 5 / 00 99 98 97 96

Table of Contents

Introduction

R amsay's noteworthy status in biblical scholarship has been recognized by historian Edwin Yamauchi: "The invaluable contributions of Sir William Mitchell Ramsay (d. 1939), the premier archaeologist of Asia Minor, to the study of the New Testament and the early church are well known."[1] From 1886–1911 he was Regius Professor of Humanity at the University of Aberdeen, his alma mater. His pioneering field work in Asia Minor advanced our knowledge of early Christianity and the Greco-Roman world. He was the author of nineteen books and scores of articles, including fifty-two entries in Hastings' four-volume *Dictionary of the Bible*. Best known among his biblical studies writings are the *Historical Commentary on the Galatians* and *The Letters to the Seven Churches*, which I recently updated (Hendrickson, 1994).

A challenge for Bible scholars and students today who seek to reference Ramsay is the inaccessibility of his writings. Most are out of print, and used copies are difficult to obtain from booksellers. Because of the datedness of his articles, few libraries contain the journals in their collections. Such is the case with the articles in this volume.

Ramsay first issued these thirty-one studies in a series called "A Historical Commentary on the First Epistle to Timothy." The studies were published in *The Expositor*, Seventh Series, 7 and 8 (1909); 9 (1910); Eighth Series, 1 (1911). The entire series was never collected and published. This is the first publication of these articles in book form. Because Ramsay does not limit his discussion to 1 Timothy but includes 2 Timothy and Titus as well, it was decided to give the work its present title. Besides, no one buys a commentary covering just 1 Timothy!

A glance at the table of contents discloses subjects that continue

7

to be relevant to scholars, pastors, and laypersons. Scholarly consensus concerning the authorship of the Pastorals has currently swung away from Ramsay's position; he strongly argues for Pauline authorship. The important role of the false teachers in Ephesus has again been highlighted by Gordon Fee in his recent commentary on the Pastorals (Hendrickson, 1988). (Indeed, I first became familiar with Ramsay's work through Fee's bibliography.) The role of women in ministry is one of today's hottest issues, and Ramsay's historical voice from outside the debate is welcome. Neither side in the current debate will be pleased with his perspective, I suspect. Regarding the church's ongoing need for effective leadership, Ramsay makes a number of important points dealing with elders and deacons.

Editorial changes in the text have been made to enhance its value for today's readers. Sentences have occasionally been modified for readability. Scripture references have been included to assist the reader. Ramsay's original translation is maintained with occasional references to modern versions. Bibliographic information in the footnotes has been expanded when available. Finally, American spelling is used.

Special thanks must be given to my assistant, Ellen Chappel, for her faithful entry of the text; to Luwanna Baker and the interlibrary loan staff at Regent University Library for persistence in securing a microfiche of the original articles; and finally Mike Bittel for the tedious task of making photocopies from the microfiche. The graduation of my son from high school and his entrance into James Madison University has provided a financial incentive to complete this project. The best of success, David!

MARK W. WILSON

1

The Purpose of 1 Timothy

The suppressed clause in the beginning of 1 Timothy (1:3) contains and conceals (so to say) the purpose which the writer had in mind. The most familiar fact to those who have to study the intimate correspondence of ancient writers possessed of literary power, such as Cicero and his friends, is the frequency of such suppression of an important verb or half sentence. The correspondent to whom the letter was addressed knew what was meant; and the suppression was due to the fact that comprehension on the part of the reader could be counted on with perfect confidence. The meaning of all such passages depends on the proper supplying of the suppressed part. Whoever cannot supply it has not penetrated to the point of view from which the letter was written; and the intention of the whole letter may be distorted, if the wrong thought is supplied. That is a difficulty which must be reckoned with: we have to go through the process of bringing ourselves into sympathy with the ancient writer by thinking afresh the thought and intention of the letter as a whole, and thus gathering what it was that the writer expected the original recipient to be familiar with, and what that first reader was expected to have in his mind as he was reading the letter.

Such a suppressed thought is a proof that the document in which it occurs is genuinely a letter, that is, the expression and product of one human soul communicating with another, sympathizing with that other, and expecting sympathetic response and comprehension. The more serious the suppression is, and the more difficult it is to supply the omitted words, the stronger is the proof that we have a real letter and not a pretended one. A forger does not express himself in this way, for he does not and cannot count on sympathetic comprehension. The forger is writing to be read by many persons, and not to be read by one alone.

9

It would not be easy to find a stronger example than the suppressed conclusion of the sentence in the third verse of chapter 1—"as I exhorted you to tarry at Ephesus"—for certain purposes which are then enumerated. What is it that Paul was going to put as the conclusion of this sentence? Timothy understood what Paul had in his mind, and the rest of the letter must show indirectly what this was. But the sentence breaks off while the writer wanders away into a description of the situation in which Timothy and the whole church at Ephesus were involved, and is then led on to point after point; and he never returns to take up the thread of the sentence. What, then, can be the conclusion of this sentence except the main purpose of the letter as a whole? Now in the letter, though the treatment of the topics is much mixed up, so that very frequently the writer touches upon some topic, diverges to another, and then returns to the former one, yet on the whole there is one guiding thought and purpose: Paul is eagerly desirous and anxious that Timothy may rightly discharge the serious duty imposed upon him, and may perfectly comprehend the difficulties that lie before him, and may know the best means of meeting them.

That this charge and duty have been committed to Timothy is emphasized repeatedly in such words as "this charge I commit unto you" (1:18), "command and teach (4:11, 5:7), "teach and exhort" (6:2). Compare also 1:3; 4:6; 5:20–21; 6:17, 20, where the same idea recurs. This charge is only temporary, to take Paul's place in his absence; but it may last a long time (3:15). The personal conduct on Timothy's part that will enable him to discharge the duty well is described in various details, especially in 4:7–8, 12–16; 5:1–4, 22–23; 6:11–13, 17, 20. Advice as to his personal conduct often passes by an easy transition into advice as to the kind of teaching which he should give (cf. 6:17–20).

The method by which Timothy will best discharge the duty imposed on him is, first, the regulation of the order and manner of public worship (2:1–2, 8–12); and secondly, the right organization of the church and of the Christian society which makes up the church on earth (3:1–13; 5:5, 9–11, 14, 16–20, 22, 24–25; 6:1–2).

The duty and charge have been imposed on Timothy by the Holy Spirit and by Paul. Prophecy marked him out and bestowed on him the gift which made him qualified for the charge, and the laying on of the hands of the presbyters had formally completed the selection and appointment (1:18, 4:14, 6:12). But the apostolic authority of Paul had also cooperated, or rather this was another aspect of the process of selection. The Spirit marked him out both through prophecy and through the apostolic power of Paul, whose apostleship made his act an expression of the Spirit's choice. Three times Paul emphasizes his authority as an apostle and herald of Jesus Christ (1:1, 12; 2:7).

This combination of the Spirit and the human authority in the same action places the thought on the same plane as that on which the book of the Acts moves (compare, e.g., Acts 13:2–3; 15:28). The point of view and outlook in the Pastoral Epistles is strikingly similar to that which we observe in the Acts. This is due to the fact that, although the Acts was composed as a single book finally about A.D. 80, yet in those parts where Luke writes on the authority of others and not on his own, it presents to us as a whole the views and needs of A.D. 57–59, when he gathered the information which he faithfully reports.[1]

The difficulties with which Timothy would have to contend in the execution of his charge are often touched upon, and evidently were constantly in the writer's mind. They will be briefly described in general terms in the following Section 4. For the present our purpose is to show that the charge imposed on Timothy is the guiding thought of the whole letter. Paul found that this thought was constantly weighing on his heart. Timothy was to take his place and was trusted to do the work which he himself did, when present, as founder and director of the church in Ephesus. It is true that Timothy had been selected because he was the suitable man for the duty. He was marked out by the Holy Spirit; he was filled with the gift and the grace of the Spirit (4:14); he had been much with Paul, and had seen Paul's manner of confirming the churches and guarding against evil and degeneration.

I do not doubt for a moment that the advice given in this letter represents just the course which Paul himself had taken often in the practical difficulties of church work, and with which Timothy had become familiar during years of companionship. It has, therefore, seemed strange and incredible to some scholars that Paul should write to urge on Timothy's attention ideas and methods which he knew so well, and his acquaintance with which was the real cause of his selection. But such scholars forget what human nature is. Paul could not shake off the thought and the anxiety about Ephesus merely because another, however much beloved and trusted, was charged with the duty. The thought of Ephesus was always with him, by day and by night. The hope that Timothy would keep all the important points in his memory, and the wish that Timothy should bear everything constantly in mind, let Paul to dictate from time to time instructions, warnings, and advice. The letter has not the appearance of having been composed at one effort, like Galatians. It is more like Corinthians (though so much shorter), having apparently been dictated in parts, according as various anxieties occurred and recurred to Paul's mind from time to time.

This vague anxiety, which was the cause of the letter, also makes it discursive. Paul's thought moves back and forwards. One topic suggests another in an undetermined and casual way. He knew that it was not necessary to write an elaborate series of instructions to Timothy, and that to compose such a formal treatise would seem almost like an intimation of distrust. Yet the anxiety always drove him on to write, to mention various details, and to intermingle expressions of his own trust in the perfection of Christ (6:14–16), of his own unworthiness of the mercy which he had found and of the authority which had been bestowed upon him (1:12–17), and other thoughts which presented themselves to his mind.

The guiding thought of the whole letter constitutes the unexpressed conclusion of the sentence in 1:3 from which we started. The protasis of that sentence, "As I exhorted you to tarry at Ephesus, when I was going into Macedonia," has for its apodosis the letter as a whole: "Therefore I send this letter to express what I would have you bear in mind, and to give suggestions from my divinely granted authority—authority bestowed upon one who was utterly unworthy of it, but still authority given fully and freely by Christ Jesus himself of his own perfect grace."

One consideration may be added to these introductory remarks regarding the purpose of this letter. Apart from Paul's natural anxiety for Timothy's success in his charge, an anxiety which prompted him to make suggestions from time to time, it was not without its advantages that Timothy should be able to refer to Paul's written word of instruction, especially if he had to differ from a member of the church older than himself. Such a person he must not rebuke, but exhort as a father (5:1). If the exhortation could be supported by quotation from a written letter bearing on Timothy's charge, it would be all the more courteous and respectful from a young man to an old man. Not that this letter has in any respect the character of a communication intended for the whole congregation under the guise of a letter to Timothy. It is the direct communication of Paul's heart with Timothy's; in it soul speaks to soul. But therein lies its effectiveness and its permanent value for the Christian world; that is what makes it so natural, so living, and so eternal in its truth.

2

The Author of the Letter

Such a letter as this could not be a forgery. It adds wonderfully to our conception of the width of Paul's mind and nature. It is quite true that, if we shut out the Pastoral Epistles, we can frame for ourselves from his other letters a picture of the remarkable and extraordinary personality from whom they emanated, and that these Pastoral Epistles stand outside of, and are not in perfect harmony with that picture. But it is not right method to assume that the narrower conception, broad and deep as it is, represents the entire breadth of Paul's nature and mind. There is revealed in the Pastoral Epistles a practical sense of the possibilities of work among common human beings, which is necessary in order to complete our comprehension of Paul's life and work. He was not merely the man who could think out the lofty theology of Romans and Ephesians, or write the exquisite panegyric on the virtue and power of love to the Corinthians, after condemning so strongly the fault and the lovelessness of individuals among them, or rebuke in such a tremendous indictment the error of the Galatian congregations. In all those letters we feel that there stands out before us a personality almost too great and too lofty for the common world of humble, low-class, immoral, vulgar paganism. We can only with difficulty understand how a Paul of that kind could ever make himself intelligible to such a world: not merely the letters but also the speech of such a man must have contained "things hard to be understood" (2 Peter 3:15) by the men and women of the pagan world. It is the Pastoral Letters which, beyond all others, show us how Paul could understand the common man, and bring himself down to the level of his needs, and how the marvelous and instantaneous effect described in the Acts and briefly mentioned in Galatians was produced by his first appearance in the Galatian cities.

Those scholars who reject the Pastoral Epistles as un-Pauline are shutting themselves off from a most valuable help to the understanding of Paul. They must, in the construction of history, suppose that there existed some such other side of Paul's nature in addition to what is shown in the greater letters. Why not accept the side as it is shown in the Pastoral Epistles?

Finally, we must take into account that the transition is easy from the one Paul to the other. There are many passages in both letters to Timothy which are conceived in the spirit and expressed in the tone of the earlier Pauline letters. There is no other writer in the New Testament to whom the two letters could for a moment be attributed. They have practically nothing in common with the other books except the one common Christian faith and practice; but they have much in common with the other Pauline letters, both in thought and in word. In the postapostolic works there is nothing which resembles them or throws any light on them.

While one must not underrate the difficulties involved in the theory of Pauline authorship, one must also remember that true scholarship is a process of triumphing over difficulties, and that the widening of knowledge means the union in one view of facts which at first sight seemed unconnected and barely consistent with each other. It is far more difficult to frame any rational theory how these letters came into existence, if they are not the work of Paul, than it is to understand them as composed by him and as completing our conception of his character.

3

Words Peculiar to the Pastoral Epistles

The totally different purpose and character of these letters from those to the Romans, Corinthians, Galatians, and other churches furnishes a partial explanation of the marked change of language and the number of new words. In all his writings Paul shows himself an innovator and a creator linguistically. To express a new system of thought he created a new method. In the Pastoral Epistles he is attempting to create a terminology that will correspond to the practical facts of an early church society in one of those rather amorphous and unorganized original congregations, which were redeemed from paganism, but not habituated to a higher plane of action and life. Many of his new words are the brief expression of something which in his earlier letters he describes as a process, but which now had become so common a phenomenon in the practical management of a congregation that it demanded a special name.

Take, for example, the very first word in this letter that is peculiar to the Pastorals. It occurs in 1:3: "I exhorted you to tarry[1] at Ephesus that you might charge certain men not *to teach a different doctrine*" (ἑτεροδιδασκαλεῖν). This fact that there were in every congregation persons, coming from without or springing up from within, who taught doctrines which Paul did not regard as healthy or right, is a fact that he in his earlier letters mentions more than once. In Galatians 1:6–9 he alludes to such teachers as preaching among the Galatian churches and says that he had warned the Galatians against them on his previous visit, that is, as early as A.D. 51. He describes the teaching in that case as the announcing of another gospel. Again, in 2 Corinthians 11:4 he describes the same thing as actually occurring in Corinth a few years later. There are persons who preach there another Jesus and a different Gospel and another Spirit. That kind of un-Pauline teaching was therefore a continual danger in the Pauline churches; and in 1 Timothy 1:3 and

6:3 it is briefly described by the single verb "to be a teacher of some different teaching." That a fact which was so frequently met with in church management should force Paul to create a single word for it is not only not un-Pauline, but is thoroughly true to Paul's mind and character.

It is not within my purpose or my power to discuss every "un-Pauline" word in the epistles; but on the whole one must feel strongly that those who label these new words as "un-Pauline" are missing a very instructive side of Paul's life and character. This single case may serve as an example of the way in which the language of Paul developed (or varied, as some may prefer to express it) with his purpose and his subject.

4

Difficulties Which Timothy Encountered in His Charge at Ephesus

The difficulties which Paul especially feared and which kept him always in anxiety for his son Timothy were of two kinds: in the first place, a false conception of Christian belief and teaching; in the second place, a wrong type of conduct and morality among the congregations.[1]

The principal passages which allude to the false conceptions of belief and thought and teaching in Ephesus and Asia generally are 1 Timothy 1:3–8; 4:1–5; and 6:3–5. Naturally this idea of the danger caused by false teaching easily turns into an emphatic statement of the importance of right teaching. The latter idea is always close to the surface of Paul's mind as he writes. His greatest anxiety is that Timothy should always give the right teaching and pronounce the right judgment in all the difficult situations and cases that come before him. This idea is very clearly stated in 1:5; 3:16; 6:6–7, 14–17. Right rule and order in the society of the church is the best preservative of truth in doctrine. Good government keeps the church active and pure.

Owing to the overwhelming importance of right teaching and the prevalence of wrong teaching, a word was coined by Paul to express in brief the process of false teaching: the thing demanded a name and a verb, as has been stated in chapter 3.

One of the errors in teaching which Paul mentions most frequently, and which he evidently hated most strongly, was the love of abstract discussions on abstruse points, verbal quibbling and logomachy, and the attention to mere words rather than the realities of life. This was the vice of education at that period: it set words and form above realities and matter. Even physical science was not experimental and practical, but consisted almost wholly in abstract theories and words. Explanations of physical and moral phenomena were frequently couched in the form of genealogies. Even the explanation of changes of name in cities or rivers, which, so far as they were real changes and did not merely rest on misapprehension, were usually due to changes in population, language, and nationality, was expressed in pseudo-historical fashion by genealogical fictions. Many examples of this way of putting history in the form of genealogical fictions may be found in the treatise attributed (falsely) to Plutarch on rivers. But the custom was not merely a late one. It was quite early, and it springs naturally from the vice of imagining that, when one has expressed a phenomenon in some new form of words, one has given an explanation of it. The subject might be traced throughout Greek thought and even earlier than Greek thought. The genealogical fiction as a substitute for history is extremely old, and is an almost universal characteristic of primitive thought.[2]

In the very ancient document incorporated in the Pentateuch as Genesis 10 we find a history and geography of the known world expressed in that form. In a choral ode of the *Agamemnon* Aeschylus expresses the moral process of degeneration through arrogant pride, and the destruction in which this degeneration inevitably ends, in the form of a genealogy.[3]

It is, therefore, unnecessary to see in Paul's mention of "fables and endless genealogies" or in his warning against teachers of a different doctrine any allusion to elaborate Gnostic theories and systems of teaching that belong to the second century. The faults against which he cautioned Timothy were rife in his own time. They sprang up naturally and quickly in the hotbed of mixed Gentile and Jewish thought, which existed in every Pauline congregation throughout the Aegean lands.

Paul regarded the tendency to quibbling and logomachy as almost the most dangerous enemy in the Greek cities like Corinth. His first letter to the Corinthians is in its first part largely prompted by the desire to combat this evil, to ridicule and to extirpate it. He perceived that the Corinthians, as they were learning a little, tended to pride themselves on their philosophic acumen; and he pointedly contrasts the simplicity of true teaching with the pretentious verbal discussion of false philosophy. Their philosophic discussions were empty and mere words: the truth was reality and power.

The "profane and old wives' fables" of 4:7, the "questionings and disputes of words" mentioned in 6:4, "the profane babblings and the antitheses of the falsely so-called knowledge," to which he so sarcastically alludes in 6:20, all bring before us what is fundamentally the same evil. That evil was rife in Corinth and in the cities of Asia. It had to be satirized and stamped out.

The words which Paul uses in his sarcastic descriptions of this evil are often peculiar to the Pastoral Epistles; but almost every time that he mentions the subject he introduces some new term; and probably, if he spoke about it fifty times, he would add a great many other terms not elsewhere employed in the New Testament. Such is the wealth of language that is characteristic of him; but the variety of his terminology is due to the intensity of his feeling on this matter.

The other class of difficulties against which Timothy would have always to contend was false morality and wrong conduct. The pagan converts had been from infancy habituated to an extremely low standard of living and speaking. It was not so difficult to stir them up on some great occasion to lofty action and noble effort, in other words, to convert them to the truth. But the real difficulty lay in keeping them up to that higher standard permanently in their everyday life. That difficulty was, for the time, insuperable. People could not suddenly throw off their earlier character and habits, and rise to a continuous new life. The old habits would constantly tend to recur. The same difficulty faces every missionary in a pagan land: conversion of individuals does not raise them in their ordinary conduct to the level of people who have behind them generations and centuries of Christian education and life (except in the case of rare and remarkable personalities). All that can be done is to raise people a little, and to trust to the effect of time and the growth of better habits in the new generations.

Throughout chapter 5 and the first half of chapter 6 especially, Paul recurs often to these faults of life, small and great, which mark the society of the Asian cities. Some of them are the faults of human nature generally, as the love of money (6:9–10), and the tendency of young widows, desiring to be married again, to gad about from house to house, and to become tattlers and busybodies (5:11–13). Others (as in 1:9–10) are of a darker kind. It is to be noticed that the faults into which the women were prone to fall are on the whole of a much slighter kind than those which were a danger to men. The standard of life was higher, apparently, among the women than among the men.

5

Date of the Epistles

That the Pastoral Epistles could not have been written by Paul during the journeys which are described in Acts may be taken as certain. It is unnecessary to repeat the arguments by which J. B. Lightfoot and others have demonstrated this. Our present aim is not to put together all that can be said about these epistles, but rather to place the reader at the point of view from which they ought to be contemplated by the historian. Regarded in the proper perspective, they are historically perhaps the most illuminative of all the Pauline epistles; and this is the best and the one sufficient proof that they are authentic compositions, emanating each complete from the mind of one author. No work whose composer makes his first object to assume the personality of another can attain such historical significance: it cannot express the infinite variety of real life unless it is written naturally and for its own sake.

Much is therefore here assumed, which is well said in every one of the many good editions on the Pastoral Epistles, sometimes with one opinion as regards authorship, sometimes with another. The impossibility of an earlier date for the letters has recently been shown more clearly by the ingenious attempts which have been made by some scholars to place them in that earlier period. Either these letters were not written by Paul, or they were written by him during a part of his life later than that which is described by Luke; that is, Paul was acquitted at the end of his two years' imprisonment in Rome and resumed his missionary work at the end of A.D. 61 or the beginning of 62.

The arguments against this later date of composition seem to be devoid of all weight. It is said that Paul shows no resentment against the imperial government on account of the massacre of A.D. 64. This argument contemplates the situation from a wrong point of view. Paul is enunciating a general principle of order in the service of the church; and he uses the generic plural "sovereigns" in the sense of "the reigning sovereign, whosoever he may be from time to time," and adds, "all who are in authority" (1 Tim. 2:2), in order to make the universality of the principle quite plain. Paul continued after 64 to think as he thought before about government. His mixed feelings towards the empire are described in the final part of the present writer's *Cities of St. Paul*;[1] but an ordered government, governors, and a people obedient to them always and necessarily formed the basis of his conception of society. Were Christians never to pray for the sovereign because Nero was a monster? Would Paul lose all his confidence in the possibilities of development in the empire for that one reason? As soon as the question is put rightly, the falsity of the argument is evident. Paul could not have interrupted his advice about the order of church service to make an exception about Nero, or to express his detestation of Nero, without ceasing to be Paul. If the letter were expressed in such a form as those who have advanced this argument demand, that would in our view be a sufficient proof that it was not written by Paul; and the same inference would probably be drawn by the very persons who have used the counter-argument.

Another argument against a date later than the period embraced in Acts is found in the absence of any reference to the great events which were taking place in Palestine from A.D. 66 onwards. This argument also shows a want of historical perspective. Why should Paul, writing in A.D. 66 or 67, be unable to compose a letter to Timothy or to Titus on subjects such as come up in these letters without alluding to the Jewish insurrection, which was now only in its initial stage? This is the *argumentum a silentio* carried to the greatest extreme that I remember to have seen. Even if Paul had been writing in 68 or 69, there is no apparent reason why he must discuss the progress of the war in these letters. But when it was barely begun, it is inconceivable and irreconcilable with the spirit of Paul's work that it should force itself into letters such as these, where Jewish matters are alluded to only in the slightest and most distant way.

A third and, at first sight, a much more reasonable argument against the hypothesis that later journeys than those described in the Acts are alluded to in the Pastoral Epistles is found in the words used by Paul himself at Miletus to the Ephesian presbyters in A.D. 57: "I know that you all, among whom I went about preaching the kingdom, will see my face no longer" (Acts 20:25). Here is apparently a prophecy which was never fulfilled. It is possible to suppose either that Paul would suggest to the presbyters the idea that he would never see them again, if this were not going to be the case, or that Luke would have recorded the prophecy if it had been falsified by future events?

In this case also this argument is based on a false conception and puts the question from a wrong and misleading point of view. As to Luke's recording the matter, we should not ask whether he would have recorded an unfulfilled and actually falsified prophecy, but whether he recorded events of history and the speeches of Paul correctly and exactly.[2] Was his intention in writing history to tell the facts as they happened, or to make out that the words of Paul and other Christians were always proved to be exact anticipations of the course of future events?

The answer to this question cannot be for a moment doubtful, except among those who start with the radically false conception of his character and of the spirit of early Christian history, against which I have been contending throughout all that I have written on this subject. Luke's object was to describe events as they happened: he was full of that sublime confidence in the facts, which animated all the great leaders of the early church. No management, no manipulation of facts, no anxiety, was required on their side: they had only to listen to the Spirit, to obey the guidance of facts, and their part was done. Success was certain without any attempt of theirs to direct the development of events. They might fail to understand the current of events at the moment, but all must be well in the end, so long as they obeyed the divine spirit implicitly. Accordingly, if Paul said he would not see the presbyters again, Luke would record this, whether or not Paul did in the issue see them again. So he records the prophecy of Agabus (Acts 21:11), though it was not exactly fulfilled; and this record has been used as evidence against him and as proof of his inaccuracy.[3] So, again, he records the two slightly varying accounts given by Paul of the details of the scene near Damascus (22:5ff.; 26:12ff.), and himself gives a third account slightly differing from both (9:3ff.), without any attempt to manipulate them into exact agreement with each other. So in the present case there is no reason to think that he would have hesitated to record Paul's forecast of the future, or that he would have refrained from telling that the brothers were specially sorrowful on account of this, even though in the future the forecast was not justified.

The question that remains, therefore, is simply whether it is possible that Paul could have made a statement to the Ephesian presbyters which even suggested anything that was not exactly and precisely in accordance with the actual course of his future action in later years. In other words, did Paul never change his plans; or were his first intentions, when once announced to anyone, like the laws of the Medes and Persians which cannot be altered? To put the question thus is to answer it. It is a mistake to regard his words as a prophecy or a forecast of the future. They are simply an explicit statement of his plan of campaign in the Roman world (already announced by Luke in 19:21).

It would be ridiculous and irrational to argue that he never changed or could change his mind. He was always guided by the current of contemporary forces, and he always seized the opportunity, even if presented unexpectedly, of the open door. He wished in autumn A.D. 50 to go from Galatia into the province Asia (doubtless to Ephesus, as Hort long ago perceived); then he planned to go into Bithynia. We can hardly doubt that he mentioned these plans to his traveling companions, and probably to the Galatian churches also. He certainly made and announced and altered plans about returning to Thessalonica in A.D. 51. In the course of his stay at Ephesus and later, he formed and announced and then changed his plans with regard to visiting Corinth (as is admitted by every scholar, with different conjectures as to the order of variation in his plans). What reason is there to think that he might not change his intentions with regard to seeing the Ephesian presbyters again? There is absolutely no reason to think so, and the change throws much light on his mind and his history, as we shall see.

But, it is maintained, the words which he uses in Acts 20:25 constitute a far more formal and solemn assurance with regard to the future than a mere announcement of plans with regard to a journey; and it seems more strange that such a serious statement as that should be belied in the event. This argument is based on a misconception of the passage, the words, and the intention. Paul, in this speech, was merely summing up and concluding the past. He (or rather Luke, who reported in briefer terms the speech) was in one word describing a wide-reaching plan, which he had had definitely and explicitly before him for more than a year.

This plan is clearly intimated both by Luke in Acts 19:21 and by Paul in several parts of the epistles to Rome and to Corinth. The plan was formed some time before he left Ephesus; and the words in 19:21 are intended to imply that it was then clearly enunciated to his friends and associates and to the churches generally. He conceived that his work in the Aegean world was now so far completed, and that the next stage was about to begin, namely, the Roman stage. He was to occupy the central city of the empire, and work there in a similar wide-reaching fashion to that in which he had worked at Ephesus. But, whereas he had at Ephesus affected the whole province Asia—a wide sphere, yet after all a restricted one—he would at Rome affect a much wider sphere. For as all the Asian cities looked to Ephesus and their citizens came sometimes to Ephesus, so the whole empire looked to Rome and all cities sent to Rome and were influenced from Rome. It was, of course, true that the wider the sphere the more attenuated was the influence exerted on the distant parts; and therefore a residence in Rome was not by itself sufficient, but would require to be supplemented by personal work in outlying regions. The East, however, had already seen Paul's face, as he thought, sufficiently. Just as he had never seen Colossae and Laodicea and Hierapolis, so (as he thought) would it now be possible for him to communicate even with Ephesus sufficiently by letter and by coadjutors. The outlying parts of the West would demand his presence more imperatively; and from Rome his intention was to go on to Spain.[4]

Such was the bold, magnificent, and statesmanlike plan which filled Paul's mind during the years A.D. 56–57. The visit to Spain was the complement of the intention not to revisit Ephesus. The two parts of the plan fitted one another, and it would be as unreasonable to argue from the words of Paul that he must necessarily have carried out the plan to visit Spain, if he lived, as it is to infer that he could not after all have revisited Ephesus, if he lived.

One thing only was needed to crown with completion his work in the four provinces of Galatia, Asia, Macedonia, and Achaia; and that was to bind these new Gentile churches into unity and brotherhood with the original church at Jerusalem. To cement that unity was a necessary part of his work; and the visit to Jerusalem was present in his thoughts from the moment when the plan began to form itself in his mind. Hence Luke, with his usual command over all the essential and critical facts of his subject, mentions it as part of the plan in his very brief account of Paul's scheme in 19:21. Paul's mind was full of this idea as he spoke to the Ephesian elders. The visit to Jerusalem was necessary to accomplish his course, though he knew that bonds and afflictions awaited him there. He must go, because he was taking with him the representatives of the churches in the four provinces and the contributions of all the congregations, to attest their unity in spirit and their sympathy in worldly fortunes with the original mother congregation in Jerusalem. Syrian Antioch had long ago been bound to Jerusalem by rendering help to the poor there in their hour of greatest need (Acts 11:29–30). Paul knew that people continue to like and take an interest in those whom they have benefited; and he trusted to the permanent effect of this charity to cement the unity of all the eastern churches, while he devoted himself to Rome and the West.

Hence, as he was starting on the voyage from Miletus to Jerusalem, he told his hearers that in accordance with the plan of work, which was well known to them, they should no longer see his face. In saying this he was addressing, not merely the Ephesians, but all the four provinces present through their delegates. It has been elsewhere pointed out that this speech passes insensibly from the narrower to the wider address, and that this change is characteristic of a real speech and inconsistent with the theory of fabrication by Luke. It is also very characteristic of Paul and suitable to the occasion. He was hereafter not to go about among these his first churches, but to work in another region. He is not here thinking of death which should divide him from them. He is not speaking as a prophet, forecasting the future. He is simply announcing the end of one stage and the entrance on a new stage. The occasion was affecting and solemn, and the words correspond to the occasion. But there is in the situation and the words nothing that in any way conflicts with the possibility that future events may have overturned Paul's plans, and that he after all found it advisable to return to his churches in the four provinces.

The question arises whether this voyage to Jerusalem was not the occasion when Paul wrote the first letter to Timothy after having left him in Ephesus before he started for Macedonia (Acts 20:1), and having again sent him to Ephesus with or after the presbyters, when they returned from Miletus to Ephesus. On shipboard, sailing from Miletus towards Jerusalem, might not Paul have composed this letter? Such is the ingenious suggestion of Mr. Vernon Bartlet. It is tempting at first sight; but, apart from other considerations, the words of 1 Timothy 4:13 are fatal to it. Paul, when he wrote this letter, was clearly purposing to come back to Ephesus and rejoin Timothy there: "Until I come, give heed to reading, to exhortation, to teaching." It is inconceivable that a few days after bidding the Ephesian presbyters farewell forever, when (as we have seen) his mind was filled with the other grandiose idea, Paul should have written to Timothy intimating the intention to come again. We can understand that future events disturbed the great plan, but we cannot understand that Paul should have within a few days changed his mind on this subject without any pressure of circumstances constraining him.

6

Organization of the Pauline Churches

The administration of his newly founded churches was a matter of the first interest to Paul. When he had been expelled suddenly from Antioch, Iconium, and Lystra in succession, and had been compelled to leave them without arrangements for their regular administration, he returned to them and completed a form of organization of a new kind more akin to the character of Hellenic cities or Roman colonies: he appointed presbyters by election.[1]

When Timothy was sent to Thessalonica during Paul's visit to Athens, he did there the same work which Paul had done in Antioch, Iconium, and Lystra, and would willingly have done in Thessalonica by returning there at the earliest possible opportunity had not Satan hindered him. That the work was done by Timothy appears from 1 Thessalonians 3:2–3: "We sent Timothy to establish you and to comfort you concerning your faith; that no one be moved by these afflictions; for yourselves know that hereunto we are appointed." Compare with this the account of Paul's work when he returned to the three Galatian cities: "Confirming the souls of the disciples, exhorting them to continue in the faith, and that through many tribulations we must enter into the kingdom of God" (Acts 14:22). The verses which follow the words just quoted from the epistle show that Paul's anxiety was that the Thessalonians should "continue in the faith." The agreement in idea and even in form between the Acts and the epistle is here so perfect that there can remain no doubt: Timothy was sent to do in Thessalonica what Paul himself went back to do in the Galatian cities.

Now Paul did something more in the Galatian churches, "And when they had appointed for them elders in every church and had prayed with fasting, they commended them to the Lord, on whom they had believed" (Acts 14:23). In the letter Paul commends the Thessalonians to the Lord (5:23) and prays for them (3:11–13), as

26

we may be sure that Timothy also had done with them. One thing remains: presbyters were chosen in the Galatian churches. Surely Timothy must have been charged to look after this matter also. There were officials who were over the Thessalonian church at the time when Paul was writing his letter. Owing to the suddenness and secrecy of his departure from the city, he could not have appointed them in preparation for that event. The apparently backward condition of the congregation in respect of knowledge and comprehension of the faith seems to show that they had not progressed so far as to be constituted into a regular church with officials before the riots broke out. Everything alike in the Acts and in the epistle points to the conclusion that all four churches—Antioch, Iconium, Lystra, and Thessalonica—were in the same condition of incomplete organization when Paul was forced to go away; and this was the reason of the extreme anxiety that Paul had felt about the Thessalonian congregation. On this account he thought it good to be left at Athens alone and to send Timothy to Thessalonica.[2]

Paul's action in those cases must be regarded as a proof of the high value that he attached to administration and government. The organization of each young church was the prime necessity, and must in one way or another be arranged.

From his earlier letters, taken by themselves, we might fail to gather that he had such a strong sense of the importance of organization and good government; and this has led many scholars to doubt the Pauline origin of the Pastoral Epistles. But the earlier letters are all suggested by special occasions and special needs. It was not part of his subject in them to lay stress on administration; yet even in them there are signs that he was quite alive to its importance. He not merely saw the overwhelming importance of unity among all the scattered churches in the one great body; he knew also that this unity could not be attained without a suitable government and mutual fitting of the parts to one another in each congregation. Each church by itself must be composed, not of absolutely homogeneous individuals, but of individuals working together for the common good in different lines; and there must be persons charged with the superintendent of the corporate life.

One single example may be mentioned, where Paul's language in a letter is guided by his sense for organization in a congregation. The church at Thessalonica was in need of further instruction on several points, about which it entertained imperfect ideas; and the first epistle was written to explain the points in question. But at the end Paul gives advice of a general kind to a young congregation in which the corporate life was still not strong (1 Thess. 5:12–22). In this advice the first thing that he lays stress on is the duty of obedience to the officials, recognition of their character, and an affectionate esteem for them on account of the work they were doing.

There is another reason why this side of Paul's mind and work has been too little noticed by many modern scholars. We have very little information about the way in which his churches were organized; and if government had been so important in his estimation, they infer that we should have known more on the subject. The little information which we possess is so obscure and conflicting, that church organization must be regarded as at that time still unimportant and merely inchoate. That the organization was in an elementary stage and that much development was still to come is of course admitted and certain; but that was inseparable from the situation. Paul took an important step in this development: he found the church in one stage, he carried it into another.

The form of government in the Pauline churches, so far as described in the Acts, was simply through presbyters. These were evidently different in character from the *presbyteroi* of the early church in Jerusalem, who apparently were not officials, but merely men of age and experience whose influence in the congregation rested, not on formal appointment or selection, but on time and wisdom. They were distinguished from the *neoteroi*, whose vigorous age was suited for the active parts of congregational work (e.g., Acts 5:6).[3] Paul's *presbyteroi* were in a true sense officers, chosen on account of their fitness and trusted with authority, as he impressed on the Thessalonians (1 Thess. 5:12), where they are called by the general term "who are over you" (προιστάμενοι). This term was probably chosen in order to convey a sense of their authoritative and governing position. That these officials were of the same kind as the presbyters in Galatia can hardly be doubted, although the word is not used. In Luke's history we must regard the first case as intended to be typical of the rest.

That the work of the presbyters was *episkope*, that is, surveillance of the common interests and corporate life of the church, cannot be doubted. As they were charged with the duty of e*piskope*, they are called *episkopoi* by Paul in Acts 20:28. That they were also teachers and preachers is a matter of course. Every Christian ought in his own way to be a teacher and preacher, when occasion offered;[4] and *a fortiori* the outstanding and distinguished Christians should be so. Now *episkope* was in Luke's estimation the duty of the apostles in the early congregation at Jerusalem (Acts 1:20). He therefore considered that the Pauline presbyters were a device for the performance, at least in part, of the duties that were discharged by the Twelve in the original congregation.

Luke does not allude to deacons in the Pauline churches. But they are mentioned in the epistle to the Philippians, where the officials are addressed as "bishops and deacons." These two kinds of officials were therefore in existence as early as A.D. 61. Now Luke regards *diakonia*, like *episkope*, as the duty of the Twelve at Jerusalem originally;[5] and it seems clear that in Luke's estimation deacons, like presbyters, performed work which fell to the apostles in the first church.

It is remarkable that, if this is so, Luke should nowhere mention the institution of deacons in the Pauline churches. And the fact becomes all the more noteworthy when we take into consideration that the general character of the views which are expressed in the letter to Timothy approximates closely to the point of view on which the book of the Acts is written. The writer of that book was entirely under Paul's influence and guidance. He had heard and learned from Paul the same ideas, with regard to the practical working of a congregation, which are here stated by the apostle to Timothy. Luke wrote with a strong sense of the importance of good administration and good government in a congregation. He traces step by step down to a certain point the growth of administrative machinery in the church, the filling up of the college of apostles, the formation of a church fund, the appointment of the Seven, the government of the church of Syrian Antioch by a college of prophets and teachers, similar in general character to the college of apostles at Jerusalem. His interest in this topic springs from his recognition of the fact that a well-governed church will be more vigorous and more healthy, and will stand on a higher level or moral character, than a badly organized one. That was also the view on which Paul worked, and his methods can never be understood unless one keeps that fact in mind.

Why, then, does Luke not mention the appointment of deacons in the Pauline churches? His silence ceases to be surprising if we take into account that his work was left unfinished. The earliest stage of the Pauline organization knew only presbyters; in the second stage deacons were added. The occasion when this development occurred was later than the arrival of Paul in Rome. That Luke, who thoroughly appreciated the importance of church organization, should intend to leave his readers with so defective a conception of it, seems as improbable as that the writer, who so well comprehended the nature of Paul's great Roman plan,[6] should bring the apostle to Rome and dismiss his further work in a brief sentence.

The relation between presbyters and deacons in the Pauline churches remains utterly obscure. It is not within Luke's purpose to tell what were the powers of duties of the presbyters. His readers were familiar with the facts of their own church; and his object was to relate what was useful for them. That there must have been some difference of function between the two classes of officials is evident. The fact that the diaconate was later in origin implies that it was intended for some purpose which previously was not satisfactorily attained. In the Pastoral Epistles there is no suggestion that higher qualifications were required for one position than for the other; yet it was inevitable that one should be less dignified than the other. The analogy of the Twelve and the Seven was not without effect. The deacons ranked in relation to the presbyters, as the Seven to the Twelve, and probably also as the *neoteroi* to the *presbyteroi* in the earliest church. Duties which required more personal effort were assigned to the deacons, as younger men. But the qualifications were practically the same, though the bishop or presbyter is more closely scrutinized because his position is the more honorable.

Nor is any quality required in a bishop or a deacon, which is not required in every Christian. The sole condition for office is that the candidate shall be approved as a thoroughly good member of the church. The deacon has the opportunity of gaining reputation and standing in the congregation. Thus he has an advantage over the ordinary Christian if he "seeks the office of a bishop" (1 Tim. 3:1). But this advantage is accidental, and there is no suggestion that the diaconate was preparatory to the office of bishop, still less that the two constituted in any way a different class or order from the mass of members of the church.

Women deacons are clearly referred to in 1 Timothy 3:11. This makes it probable that the diaconate was not in the same way an office as the position of bishop or presbyter was.[7] It carried with it no authority in the church. It was in itself only a burden; but the person selected to bear the burden was thereby honored, and the eyes of all were on the deacon. As being thus regarded by all, a true deacon was likely to be stimulated to the fullest performance of the duties of a true Christian.

The meaning of the regulation in 3:2, 12 and 5:9 has been much discussed. But beyond question it means only "monogamistic" in the fullest and purest sense. It neither forbids second marriage nor enjoins marriage. The writer of the Pastoral Epistles did not differ in this respect from the writer who praised celibacy and devotion to the divine life when he wrote to the Corinthians. This point needs no elaboration. It is insisted on by Paul merely because he had to emphasize the higher standard of moral purity in the Christian church. Every Christian, and not merely a bishop, must be strictly monogamistic.

While the presbyterate of the Pastorals[8] is clearly an office of authority in the congregation, there is no reason to think that the authority rested on the office in itself. The honor in which the presbyter was held is based on the way in which the office was filled, just as it is in 1 Thessalonians 5:12. The presbyter had authority in certain departments of congregational life. He ought to be regarded with loving honor on account of his work, because he convinced others by his deeds that he deserved honor. He was officially a teacher, but all Christians taught; all spoke and prayed in the assembly. The older members of the church were regarded with honor. Even Timothy ought not to reprove a person older than himself. The bishop, as Paul desires to see him, is simply the best and most typical Christian in the congregation, and honor is paid to him on that account.

The organization of the church in the Pastoral Epistles, therefore, is not apparently advanced one step beyond that of the church in Philippi in A.D. 61. We have in them the Pauline church as it was in the later years of Paul's life, whether or not he survived the first trial in Rome. But we see no reason to doubt for a moment that he survived it, and returned to the Aegean lands and churches.

The Pastoral Epistles show us a series of glimpses into the management and the actual condition of the Pauline churches in the Aegean world. The demand for obedience and respect to the officials was urgently needed. Disorder was rife in the congregations. The struggle to establish the authority of the officials continued throughout the first century; and its later stage appears in Clement's epistle to the Corinthians.

7

The False Teachers

The teachers, whose action in the Asian cities Paul dreaded and urged Timothy to resist, were evidently members of the congregations. Their intentions were in themselves not reprehensible. They felt prompted to speak and to teach; and they gave expression to their views, since it was customary for any of the brethren to speak in the assembled congregation as the Spirit moved them, both men and women. Scenes of disorder were apt to arise if several spoke simultaneously; and Paul had to repress the unseemliness of such public appearances. He especially discouraged the women from speaking in the congregation, though, of course, considering what his views were as to the free action of the Holy Spirit and as to the quality of all human beings—Jew and Gentile, slaves and free persons, male and female, in the presence of God—it was impossible for him to go so far as positively to forbid any woman whom the Spirit moved to speak. But he could, and did, forbid them to teach and to hold an office of authority over men.

But the teachers, whom he has in mind in this letter, were persons who went beyond mere speaking in the public assembly, and set up as professional teachers or lecturers. He accuses them of desiring to make money by their teaching, "supposing that godliness is a way of gain" (6:5). Now Paul did not think that it was wrong for the teachers or evangelists in the church to be paid and maintained by the church. On the contrary, he entirely approved of this custom and defended it. There is no reason to think that the writer of the Pastoral Epistles differed from Paul and disapproved of such payment. He is referring to another matter. These teachers whom he disliked so much were not the regularly chosen officials of the congregation, but volunteers, who set up as teachers with the intention to make a business and a means of livelihood out of the Word of God: "the falsely-called knowledge, which some professing[1] have erred" (6:21). In Titus 1:11

the phrase "for filthy lucre's sake" is directed against the same class of persons. But the English version is open to misunderstanding, as if all lucre, that is, pay gained by teaching, were disgraceful. It is only money gained by bad or false teaching that is disgraceful; and the passage might be rendered, "who make a gain that is dishonorable by teaching what they ought not."

We are here placed in view of Christian society in a certain stage of its development. The historical question is whether this stage is a very early one or whether it belongs to the end of the first century or even to the middle of the second century, which is the date that some have assigned for the composition of the Pastoral Epistles. It obviously would not be possible that at the time when Paul was writing Galatians or Thessalonians, difficulties of this kind would be of such serious importance that his attention should be largely directed to them. In that first stage of the growth of a newly founded congregation matters of that kind would be comparatively unimportant. Paul's attention in that stage is mainly directed (1) to making his own doctrine clearer and better understood by the congregations, (2) to combating the doctrine of missionaries coming in to preach a doctrine opposed to his own and in his opinion fundamentally false and fatal, and (3) to rebuking, correcting, and punishing moral faults and vices among his converts, faults largely arising from the persistence in them of their original pagan standard of morality and conduct. That third class of difficulties is similar to one of the two classes which are chiefly treated in 1 Timothy (see chapter 4). The others hardly appear in the Pastoral Epistles.

These amateur and volunteer teachers to whom Paul refers were setting up in their own congregation, and could have some hope of gaining a livelihood. That implies a Christian society and social character already formed in the congregation. The congregation must therefore have existed for some time. Can we suppose that, before Paul's death in A.D. 66, or at latest 67, his congregations in the Hellenic cities were already so far developed that rival teachers, official and unofficial, were in a way competing with one another? I confess that this state of the congregations, so far from being of later character, seems to me to suit only with an early stage in their development, and to be irreconcilable with a second-century date. The only question is whether it belongs to A.D. 65 or to A.D. 90. I shall try to show that there is no reason why it should not exist between 60 and 70, though it doubtless continued for some time. It was extirpated by establishing firmly the authority of the officials and forbidding all amateur teachers; and Clement's epistle to the Corinthians derives its importance largely from its having been accepted as settling finally the principle of obedience to the church officers as such.

8

The False Teachers and Their Place in the Early Church

In the preceding chapter the attempt has been made to put clearly the question regarding the position in the church of the false teachers, whom Paul describes in the Pastoral Epistles. That the same class of teachers is alluded to in all three epistles is universally admitted; and we have assumed it from the outset.

There is not the slightest ground for classing these false teachers along with the great leaders and teachers of heresies in the second and later centuries. Paul's attitude to them is totally different from that of the church leaders in that subsequent period to the heretics and the heresiarchs; and his description of the false teachers contains little that suits those heretic leaders, while it contains a good deal that is inconsistent with those later heretic sects and their founders. The Pastoral Epistles set before us a time in which almost everything connected with the church is still fluid and inchoate. Organization, administration, the order and manner of church service, etc., are not yet settled, but are only in process of evolution. On the other hand the heretics of the second century diverged from an already established rule and order, and were regarded by their orthodox opponents as doing so.

The Pastoral Epistles should be interpreted throughout on this plane of inchoateness. They refer to the circumstances of a growing, not of a fixed and matured, church. The words of the writer are pregnant with meaning, and yet one must not everywhere insist too much on the words. The circumstances to which they referred were sometimes only the incomplete stage of something which should hereafter become fixed and definite, sometimes perhaps obsolescent and about to give place to another more permanent fact.

The preceding paragraph must not be understood as detracting in any way from the continuity and uniformity of developing that characterized the early church. The present writer is as strongly convinced as anyone can be that the church in the first century is an example of singularly regular growth and that the germ of almost everything in the second-century church can be traced in the earliest stages of that church's history. The development was, in a sense, natural and inevitable; the seed grows into the tree. But the development was inevitable only in the environment: it would have been stunted or altered in a different environment. Paul, who watched over and in an exceptional degree guided—so far as humans could be said to guide—that development, considered that it was accomplished in a perfectly normal way, according to its own nature. It happened because the environment of the Roman Empire was suitable for it, because the purpose and will of God had selected that time and those surroundings, because "when the fullness of time came, God sent forth his Son." Such was his opinion at an earlier date, when he was writing to the Galatians (4:4; cf. 1:15–16) and to the Ephesians (1:10); and there is no reason to think he had changed his mind one whit in this regard when he wrote to Timothy. It is quite evident that he was, if possible, more firmly convinced than ever of the truth of his own earlier view.

Now, however, he saw more clearly the difficulties of the case. In the course of his own experience he had learned more easily and quickly to appreciate the external difficulties and the way of meeting them. But the internal difficulties were always present to him, and they seemed only to grow more numerous, more aggravated and more dangerous as time passed. In each stage of the growth of the church, as one internal difficulty was surmounted, there seemed to arise others greater and worse. Human nature was subject to an endless series of errors. The weakness, the follies, and the earlier habits of the young converts were always asserting their power. Even the excellences of individuals were liable to turn into faults and to produce dangers. The Jewish Christians, who formed an appreciable, though usually a small, part in all those congregations of the Aegean and the Anatolian lands, started their life in the church on a much higher platform of moral knowledge, if not always of moral practice, than the ordinary pagan converts. But in different ways there were as many and as grave dangers from the former as from the latter class of members.

Anxieties like these were always weighing heavy on Paul's spirit, and prompted the warnings and advice on points of detail as they occurred to him, which he noted down and sent to Timothy in the first epistle. The warnings are sometimes, apparently, rather disjointed and unconnected; but they have a real connection in the nature of Paul's mind, always pondering over and sympathizing with the difficulties to which his converts and his coadjutors were exposed. They are strung on the thread of his own personal character: they follow the order in which his mind recurred to them. Nor does this anxiety as to Timothy's success in his difficult task imply any unfairness or too great mistrust of Paul's comrade of many years. Paul would doubtless have felt the same anxiety about his own success in that task: he was often distressed and terrified respecting his power of accomplishing the work that lay before him: "He was afflicted on every side: without were fightings, within were fears" (2 Cor. 7:5). If we had his own meditations and his warnings to himself, we should probably find that he often gave himself counsels of the same kind that he gives to Timothy.

Among those difficulties that Timothy had to face, the false teachers seem to have aroused the most apprehension in Paul's mind, if we may argue from the frequency with which they recur in the epistles. Either they were a very serious danger, or Paul was afraid lest Timothy might be unable to stand against them. They were clever in specious reasoning, fluent in words, and confident in their own powers, whereas Timothy was rather timid and distrustful of himself, and in all probability neither very highly educated nor very smart as a speaker. There was, therefore, serious danger lest they might intimidate and browbeat him, and thus obtain the mastery in the Asian congregations. A boy brought up in so remote and rude a colony as Lystra was not well equipped by his early training for facing such opponents as those false teachers. They were all the more dangerous because they were not open enemies. They do not seem to have taught anything consciously opposed to the fundamental truths of Christianity. They were members of the congregation. They were obeying in their own way the precept of Paul, and the opinion universal in the church of that time, that every Christian should be a teacher. It was difficult for the less nimble-witted Timothy to cope with their quick and well-trained intellects.

To get some clearer idea as to the character, position, and profession of those teachers, we must of course begin by putting together all that is said about them in the Pastoral Epistles. That has been already done in many excellent books, and need not be formally repeated here.[1] But it is necessary also to interpret these scattered allusions, and to reconstruct the figure from the fragmentary details. The reconstruction must be made in the light of all that is known about the social conditions of such cities as Ephesus at that period; and it is inevitable that a certain element of subjective opinion should be applied in the process. The picture which we draw cannot be proved to be certain in all its details; and it will be least convincing to those who are thoroughly familiar with the accepted views about Greek cities and Greek society in the classical period without going on to study carefully the scanty evidence regarding the Hellenistic cities of Asia in the century before and after Christ. There are profound differences between the society of Athens in the fifth and fourth centuries B.C. (as we all learn about it for many years at school and college) and the society of such a town as Ephesus in the time of St. Paul. Many details of the later life assume a different aspect to, and are misinterpreted by those who have too thoroughly and exclusively saturated themselves with the other Greek knowledge. It is more really useful to compare the Ephesus of the period in question with the educated Roman society of the early empire, for education at Rome in that period was largely Hellenistic in character.

We must in the outset lay down as our guiding principles (1) that the early Christian churches in the Aegean lands did not cut themselves off from the education of their own time, and (2) that the education of their time was (as described in chapter 4) far too exclusively given up to words, and too little concerned with the study of real things. The early Christian churches in the Aegean lands consisted largely of the energetic middle classes, who were comparatively well-to-do through their industry and trade, and who were favorably disposed towards education (as the Hellenic race always has been and still is) and able in their comfortable circumstances to have leisure for acquiring education.[2] In Paul's first epistle to the Corinthians (1:18ff.) he shows his fear that already at that early stage in its history the church of Corinth was dangerously prone to philosophic and dialectic display. In writing to the Colossians (2:8) he warns them "to let no one make them a prey through the philosophy which is an empty deceit." The same danger existed in those churches, which fills him with growing anxiety later when he was writing the Pastoral Epistles. In every pagan social gathering of which we know any details, the guests prided themselves on making some show of their interest in and knowledge of literature or mythology or philosophy. There is no reason to think that the Christians were free from this foible—which has its good side as well as its bad side. They were people of their time, with its faults and its excellences; and from St. Paul's letters we gather that they had a liberal share of its faults.

It must also be remembered what a large and important part was played in the society of the period by teachers of philosophy. When all classes of the population, which were sufficiently well off to have any leisure, loved to make some show of education and skill in literary and philosophic discussion, it is evident that there was abundant opening for teachers of philosophy in every city. To illustrate the language of the Pastoral Letters about the false teachers, we turn to the writers who describe the society of the first century— Petronius, Suetonius, Juvenal, Statius, Martial, etc.—and we recognize the same general type in a character often mentioned by them. This character was one which has no exact modern counterpart. The class of persons described by those writers present certain features corresponding to many different classes of persons in modern society: schoolmasters, private tutors, popular lecturers, university professors, Sunday school teachers, professional entertainers in social meetings, preachers. They have some of the features of each, but all the features of none. They were of the most varied kind and type themselves, from men of the loftiest moral standard ever attained in pagan society to persons little above vulgar magicians or buffoons. They were usually foreigners in Italy, coming from Greece or the Greek-speaking cities of Asia; and native-born Italians tried to compete with them but failed lamentably in the competition.

Take, for example, Juvenal's picture, bearing in mind his tendency to exaggerate (in which respect he is perhaps worse than any other writer that has ever won literary fame) and to paint in black and detestable colors. The words which have been used above about the false teachers in Ephesus and other Aegean cities—"clever in specious reasoning, fluent in words, and confident in their own powers"—might almost be regarded as an unconscious translation of Juvenal's words about the Greeks who crowded into Rome, coming from Samos, Trallis, Alabanda, and other cities of Asia and islands of the Aegean Sea: *ingenium valox, audacia perdita, sermo promptus* (*Satires* 3.70ff.).[3] Their quick intellect, unblushing self-confidence, and ready oratory made them far too clever for the more slow-witted and less versatile Romans to cope with. Many other features are common to the two pictures. Both Paul and Juvenal give a bad account of the moral character of those persons, of their false pretenses, and of the influence which they exerted on the households and families into which they were admitted, and the way in which they gained their influence. According to Paul, they were corrupted in mind (1 Tim. 6:5; 2 Tim. 3:8). They "creep into houses and take captive silly women laden with diverse lusts, ever learning and never able to come to the knowledge of the truth" (2 Tim. 3:6–7); "evil men and impostors[4] shall wax worse and worse" (2 Tim. 3:13); "they overthrow whole houses, teaching things which they ought not for filthy lucre's sake" (Titus 1:11); "giving heed to seducing spirits and doctrines of devils through the hypocrisy of men that speak lies, branded in their own conscience as with a hot iron" (1 Tim. 4:1–2)[5]: in the congregations people "will heap to themselves teachers after their own lusts; and will turn away their ears from the truth and turn aside unto fables" (2 Tim. 4:3–4; Titus 1:14). Juvenal tells how they insinuate themselves into wealthy households, where they become dear and intimate friends (*Satires* 3.72).[6] They are teachers of literature or oratory, physicians or magicians who adapt themselves to every humor of their patrons with cunning hypocrisy. They practice on the vices and weaknesses of every member of the household and betray their own pupils to death (3:16). As Paul consigns them to Satan (1 Tim. 1:20), Juvenal loathes the very city where they have settled (*Satires* 3.60).

Paul dwells most on those sides of their character which he found most dangerous to his converts; Juvenal describes with special care either what was ugly and repulsive (so that his words often defy quotation), or the qualities which aided their competition with himself as a humble friend in the same household, whom they completely outshone in the estimation of the family. It would be easy to complete the analogy by quoting from other writers of the period (and from other passages in Juvenal) characteristics of these Greek teachers corresponding to every trait which Paul mentions, for example, the kind of teaching that they gave in mythology, empty verbal dialectic, pretentious moral theories about the simple and ascetic life (in striking contrast with the conduct of the teachers). The striking feature of difference lies in the teaching of celibacy, to which Paul refers, and to which I cannot quote any sufficient parallel. But this difference brings us to the consideration of an apparent difference in nationality. Paul several times mentions the Judaistic character of the false teaching (1 Tim. 1:7; 4:3, 8; Titus 1:10, 14–15; 3:9). The teaching of celibacy springs from a mixture of Oriental with Western speculation and teaching. The speculative teachers in the Pauline churches found a special source of inspiration and profit in the weaving of theories which affected a synthesis of Hebrew and Greek thought. That sort of speculation was readily received in the early church, where everyone who could think was thinking about the relation between the Jewish and the Christian teaching, between the law of Moses and the doctrine of Christ.

But such differences of teaching existed necessarily in different localities. The teachers adapted themselves to the varying requirements of different people. There is no reason to doubt that similar differences would be observable between the pagan teachers in different regions, and even in different households of the same city. Where the teacher found a place in a Roman family that was interested in Oriental ideas and perhaps practiced the worship of Sabazios or of Isis, he adapted himself to the tastes of his hearers. Theories which brought together Western and Eastern ideas and myths and deities were fashionable and frequent in the imperial time. Juvenal speaks chiefly of Greek teachers; but he really has in mind those Hellenistic teachers whose language was Greek, although they were often Syrian or Egyptian or Cilician by birth. The Stoic teacher whom he describes as having betrayed his own pupil to death was a native of Berytos (Beirut), and he says that Rome was full of Syrians and Syrian vices (*Satires* 3.116, 166).

In short, we must conclude that the false teachers of the Pastoral Epistles are only a species of the general class of popular instructors and lecturers who were found over the whole Roman world throughout the imperial period. The species adapted itself to the local conditions and the tastes of their patrons. These teachers taught for the sake of earning a livelihood or making a fortune, not because they were filled and inspired with the knowledge of the truth and compelled to utter the knowledge which burned in their hearts. They had not been selected by the congregations to be officials and teachers. They were volunteers, and they had to seek pupils by specious arts, by teaching what would make them popular, even (as Paul declares) by practicing on the superstitions and on the vices of the weak and foolish.

In this there is nothing that is inconsistent with the period A.D. 60–70. It is probable that the letter to the Colossians briefly refers to teachers of the same class, though this opinion may be disputed by some scholars, who would prefer to regard the Colossian heretics as missionaries coming in to combat the Pauline doctrine. However that may be, the picture given in the Pastoral Epistles is sufficiently detailed to give certainty. The teachers there described may be placed quite as probably in A.D. 65 as in A.D. 95; and the fluid, unformed condition of the congregations forbids us absolutely to put the epistles later than the first century.

In illustration of the readiness with which such teachers might find an opening in the early church, we must not forget that Paul and other missionaries, when they entered for the first time into one of those cities of the Aegean lands, appeared to the population in the same character as volunteer lecturers in philosophy and morals. It was expected that, as soon as they had acquired popularity and were sought after, they would begin to charge fees and make money. And Paul maintains that the teacher who gave right teaching was worthy of being paid, though he himself preferred always to give his instruction free, and rather to earn his living by manual labor and to teach only in the intervals of working.[7]

The exaggerated picture which Juvenal draws of the moral character of the Greco-Asiatic teachers whom he describes cannot, of course, be applied to the false teachers in the Ephesian and other Asian congregations. His picture is false even about Roman society. He was an exaggerator by nature as well as by intention and habit. He took the occasional evils and described them as the normal character of the teachers, whom he hated as successful rivals. But further, many and serious as were the faults of the converts in Paul's churches, those congregations represented a distinctly higher level or moral life and conduct than ruled in ordinary pagan society. Hence Paul's picture lacks the blackness of Juvenal's. He alludes to moral faults in the Ephesian teachers; but when his statements are carefully read, the worst moral features are seen to be more in the future than in the present. The evils are going to be the result of special and conceited theorizing, but there is no reason to think that they were all existent already. Paul is rather uttering warnings than denouncing crimes.

Some scholars find that there is a difference of tone in the three Pastoral Epistles towards the false teachers, and that this difference cannot be explained in any other way than as a consequence of the progressive development of the false teaching. If the view stated above is even approximately correct, there was no single heresy, with a definite tendency and line of development of its own; and therefore there can be no possibility of explaining the difference in Paul's tone toward the false teachers by the development and growing intensity of its peculiar system of error. There was, as we think, no system of error; there was only an unregulated and therefore dangerous habit of using opportunities for gaining a livelihood by specious and unstable teaching. The false teachers had no common doctrine except the Christian faith, which they were united in assuming to be true; but they had no right understanding of it in itself, or of the Mosaic Law, or of the relation between the two. The cure lay in supplying right teaching in place of this haphazard and capricious teaching; and this was possible only through better organization and regulation of the congregation and through steady insistence on the right doctrine, which ought to be consistently placed before learners by all teachers.

Here, as everywhere in the study of the Pastoral Letters, everything depends on the point of view; and the champions of the opinion and argument which we have just alluded to have been misled by the presumption, which underlay their thought from the beginning, that there was a definite school of heretical doctrine against which the writer of the three epistles is directing all his efforts. In fact, we find that in this, as so often is the so-called "higher criticism," the entire position is assumed in the outset: grant the preliminary assumption, and the rest follows with unerring logic. If the foundation is safe, the rest of the building is often faultless and lasting. Unfortunately, we hold the preliminary assumption to be wrong, and the foundation of the structure to be unstable as a quicksand.

How then explain the difference of tone in the epistles? The slight difference of tone is due to subjective, not to objective causes. It arose in Paul's mind and nature, and was not forced on him by external circumstances and by the more defined and alarming character of the false teaching. The view against which we are contending is that in 2 Timothy the danger is least, the condemnation mildest, and the heresy vaguest and least sharply defined. Titus occupies a middle position; and in 1 Timothy there is the sharpest and clearest definition, the strongest condemnation, and the most vivid apprehension of the danger. The conclusion from this statement of the facts is that 2 Timothy was composed last, and 1 Timothy first of the three epistles. The case for the authenticity of the Pastoral Letters is thereby annihilated, for they allude to historical facts in the opposite order. In 1 Timothy Paul is free and planning further travels and missionary enterprises; in 2 Timothy he is in prison, and his condemnation and death are imminent. If 2 Timothy is a genuine writing of Paul's, it is almost the last expression of his wishes in life. From this again it follows that the writer deliberately and intentionally took on himself the character of Paul, and placed his letters successively in certain situations of Paul's life, inserting references to the circumstances of the apostle in order to give verisimilitude to the letters and to cheat readers into the belief that they were composed by the founder of the Ephesian and other Aegean churches, and thus to gain increased authority for his statement of his own views.

As to the difference of tone between Titus and 1 Timothy, the case seems to me to break down entirely. I see none. The one letter is a much briefer statement of advice which is practically on the same stage as the warnings and counsel given in the other.

The difference in tone between 1 and 2 Timothy is extremely interesting. It is the difference between the tone of a fighter in the midst of a keen struggle and the tone of the same man on his deathbed. The earlier letter is the harder, sharper, and more threatening expression of the combatant; whereas 2 Timothy is the milder and gentler word of him whose warfare is over. But even in 2 Timothy the tone is every whit as serious. Paul regards the danger in as grave a light as formerly; but he does not condemn his present opponents so sharply. He rather insists on the future consequences that will result from their line of action and teaching. In a sense, the condemnation expressed in 2 Timothy 3:1–9 is as uncompromising as anything in 1 Timothy. The dying apostle has not relaxed a whit in his warfare against error and wrong. But on the whole there is a gentler tone in the last letter, and a firmer conviction that the evil is evanescent and that the right will win. This difference in tone, misunderstood by an unsympathetic judgment contemplating the facts from a false point of view, is the foundation for an imposing but perishable structure of theory.

The false teachers of Ephesus interest us both as a stage in the history of education, and as a moment in the development of organization and discipline in the church. But they play no part and have no importance in the development of doctrine, for they do not represent a heretical moment or system as their teaching was the result of a tendency of human nature. They present certain analogies to the Sophists in Athens in the fifth century B.C. Like the Sophists they were a heterogeneous aggregate of individual teachers, having no common system of thought to form them into a class, but having a common aim, namely, to make a livelihood and a reputation by teaching, and seeking this aim by methods similar in the different cases because they were suggested by the circumstances of the situation and by the nature of human beings. It is always the case that such volunteer teachers, competing with one another, are tempted to seek for popularity by accommodating themselves to the weaknesses of the people whom they seek to attract. Individual teachers resist this temptation, and if they are possessed of strong character and endowed with considerable powers in their profession, they may not suffer from their resistance, but win success and be respected all the more because they have resisted a serious temptation. But the temptation is too strong for many of the competitors, especially for the weaker ones. It is easy to find much to say in defense alike of the Sophists and of the Ephesian false teachers; but the fact remains that both were condemned on similar grounds by the greatest of thinkers and moralists in their own time. And history must pronounce the decision that they were a dangerous phenomenon in the development of society and education.

In the development of organization in the church the false teachers also had a distinct importance. How was this danger to be met? So far as Paul could see, the cure lay in stricter discipline within the church, and in placing the teaching more exclusively under the care of persons approved by the choice of the congregation after scrutiny of their character and knowledge and doctrinal position. For this purpose organization must be systematized and strengthened, and the virtue of obedience to authority must be inculcated. That is the general subject and tendency of the Pastoral Letters, as contrasted with the earlier Pauline letters; and it is this characteristic which most brings their authenticity under suspicion. Yet the development in Paul's views seems natural and necessary, if he lived long enough, that is, if he was not condemned to death at the first Roman trial. There is always in every spiritual and intellectual movement the same sequence: first, the insistence on the individual freedom and the individual right to live his own intellectual and moral life. Then the realization by experience of the other truth, that man is not really free when he is left too much to individual caprice, that he attains true freedom best under the reign of law, and that the virtue of obedience must be cultivated carefully, because only through obedience does one learn to be free, and only by obeying the law can one attain to freedom from the law. Such is the lesson that we who are engaged in the practical work of education at the present day in this country are learning, and we have learned it sufficiently. Many teachers who have lived long enough must be conscious of having gone through a similar development of view and method to that which is observed in the earlier epistles and in the Pastoral Epistles of Paul.

As we have stated above, much can be said in defense of the false teachers; and when we scrutinize the three letters carefully, we find that Paul's condemnation is stronger of the results and future consequences of their teaching than of their actual present character. The moral evils that originate from them are rather contingent and future than actual and present. Their influence on "silly women, laden with sins" (2 Tim. 3:6)[8] is a feature that looks very ugly, especially when one thinks of the character and faults of ancient life. But we must bear in mind that, in that stage of religious development, it is the more emotional and frivolous who are most easily led into extremes of fantastic and emotional religiosity. Paul foresaw the prospect that various abnormal types of an overexcited and enthusiastic religious devotion might acquire a hold on that kind of women whose feelings were stronger than their judgment. In guarding against this he insists on the need for inculcating a norm and rule and law. Yet a careful weighing of all the references of the epistles certainly point to the result that the apostle was taking this danger at a very early stage, and did not allow it to grow serious before he began to organize precautions against it. The epistles belong to an early stage—a very early stage indeed—in church history.

Only in this interpretation of their meaning and purpose can we reconcile the evidence about Ephesus contained in the two letters to Timothy with the strong and hearty testimony which the Revelation and the letter of Ignatius bear to the services rendered by the Ephesians in detecting and rejecting false teachers, and to their career of patient truth and steadfast love "for my name's sake."[9] The evidence from widely different sources works into the one uniform picture, when all is rightly contemplated.

There are two questions which insistently present themselves on this subject. Was St. Paul's opposition to these teachers successful? And, if so, what was likely to be the effect on Christian society?

That his opposition was successful seems beyond question. The authority of the officials appointed in each congregation gradually established itself, and was fully and generally recognized early in the second century. The volunteer teachers' profession seems to have decayed and disappeared in the church. The results were unfortunate: the counsel given in the Pastoral Epistles was regarded as complete and final, whereas it ought to have been treated as only the beginning of legislation. The epistles readily open to be misinterpreted in the sense that Christian teaching should be in the hands, or at least under the control, of the church officials (presbyters or bishops and deacons then, bishop with presbyters and deacons later). In the Lycaonian church of the fourth century it would appear almost that the priests were the only teachers; at least, the office of teaching is mentioned in various epitaphs as if it were an important and necessary part of their official duties.[10]

Bigg, in his singularly able, learned, and suggestive book, points out that the education of Christian children lay largely in the hands of pagan teachers.[11] This proves that the discouragement of the volunteer teachers was successful, and that the substitution of clerical in place of lay teaching (which was practically the result, though these terms "clerical" and "lay" anticipate the actual facts of the second century, and are therefore rather anachronistic) was unable to supply the educational needs of the congregations. The needed supplement to the Pastoral Epistles was the establishment of an educational system in Christian society. The task was too great.

The forces of the empire were against it. The tendency was for education to degenerate and disappear. Despotism in government, apathy among the governed, increasing rigidity of caste and class distinctions in society, the system of cheap amusements and charitable feeding of an idle and uneducated proletariat were destroying the empire. Very few among the leaders of the church in post-Pauline times felt the needs and the value of education in Christian society. None attained to a statesmanlike conception of the nature, causes, and cure of the evil. Whether Paul, if he had lived, would have met the situation cannot be known. He was cut off immediately after the Pastoral Letters were written; and their purpose was narrowed and hardened in the estimation of subsequent generations.

9

Two Examples of the False Teachers

In 1 Timothy 1:20 two individual false teachers, Hymenaeus and Alexander, are mentioned, and Paul's condemnation of them is described. But the brevity of the allusion is such that doubt might be felt whether it is as false teachers or for some totally different cause that they are mentioned here. But the doubt is unnecessary. The false teachers and the antidote to their influence on the Asian congregations is the guiding thought throughout the epistle; and it continually recurs to Paul's mind, without any formal connection with the preceding thought. Moreover, Hymenaeus is again mentioned in 2 Timothy 2:17 as a false teacher, and the doctrine which he and Philetus taught is described briefly: "who concerning the truth have erred, saying that the resurrection is past already, and overthrow the faith of some." This is evidently a popular philosophical explanation of the idea of the resurrection, an idea which seemed so irrational and absurd to the ordinary Gentiles that Festus called Paul a fool for speaking about it seriously (Acts 26:23–25). And the Athenian audience in the court of Areopagus, when he mentioned it, either mocked or politely postponed the further hearing to some remote and more convenient time (Acts 18:31–32).[1]

Inevitably the Christianized Hellenes must have begun to speculate, to theorize, and to frame philosophic explanations of this doctrine, which was to them so incomprehensible, almost as soon as they became Christians. One such rationalistic explanation is alluded to in the *Acts of Paul and Thekla* (§14)[2] as being current in Paul's lifetime and reprobated by him; namely, that the resurrection of the dead is merely an expression for the continuity of the household, and that the parent lives again in the children. This explanation is so natural and so much in accordance with the old religious thought of Asia Minor[3] that it was sure to be suggested in Christian circles at a very early date, and the statement of the *Acts* that it was current during the life of Paul probably preserves a true tradition.

What was the exact form of allegory or theory, by which Hymenaeus explained away the resurrection into some idea that was embraced in the shallow philosophy current in educated society of that period, is not specified by Paul. Timothy knew the teaching which he had in mind, and therefore there was no need to describe it more fully. Here we need not offer any conjecture about it. It is sufficient to recognize that it belonged to a type of philosophic theorizing which must have been current at the earliest period in the Hellenic congregations; and that it was just the sort of teaching which was likely to be in the mouths of the class of false teachers whom we have described.

Paul's treatment of Hymenaeus and Alexander was stern: "whom I delivered unto Satan that they might be taught not to blaspheme" (1 Tim. 1:20). What is the meaning of this penalty, which is so remote from our way of thinking and speaking? Probably it expresses an idea which is alien to modern and Western minds, and can hardly be understood by us; but we can see at least part of what was meant. The often-discussed passage, 1 Corinthians 5:3–5, refers to a similar penalty, but the manner of it is, if possible, more obscure. The penalty in that case was inflicted, not on a false teacher, but on one who had been guilty of an extremely gross moral offense. "For I, at all events, being absent in body but present in spirit, have already, as if really present, formed the decision in respect of him that has so wrought this thing, in the name of the Lord Jesus, you being gathered together and my spirit, in association with the power of the Lord Jesus, to deliver such a one unto Satan for the destruction of the flesh, that the spirit might be saved in the day of the Lord."

In both cases it is important to observe that the punishment is not merely vindictive, but reformatory. Its purpose is "that the spirit may be saved," so "that they might be disciplined not to blaspheme." The means of punishment is through bodily suffering and even death. The phrase "for the destruction of the flesh" in the one case shows what sort of discipline is indicated in the other. The analogy to a common usage in the religious and social custom of Asia Minor is so close and evident that we cannot neglect it. Paul and his readers knew this custom too well to miss the likeness. He must have been conscious of it, and they must have recognized it in his words. One who had sinned against the god or the goddess was punished with some disease (usually fever) or some bodily suffering or loss of some part, and no cure was possible until the sin was admitted and expiated. Numerous "confessions," inscribed on stone and deposited in or near the sanctuaries of Asia Minor, have been found which record the sin, the suffering, the repentance, the pardon, and the acknowledgment of the divine power and law.[4]

The analogy, though striking, is not complete. In the first place, the pagan belief was that the deity interfered and punished the sin. Paul and the church,[5] in association with the power of God made manifest to humanity, consigned the criminal to Satan. But here we must recognize that Satan is merely the instrument which the power of God employs to chastise and to teach the criminal: the criminal is not placed eternally under Satan's power, but only for a season and for a purpose.

In the second place, Paul acts with authority and power. He calls in the power of evil, and hands over the criminal to that power. It is true that he does this in the name and under the authority of Jesus, but he appears to human eyes as the agent, and the power of Jesus is an unseen influence acting through him and with him. In the pagan custom either some person who has suffered through the criminal's act invokes the god, or the god acts on his own initiative. No human being has any power or authority: that belongs to the god alone, and any person who intervenes does so as a suppliant. This is a real and deep difference, but it stands in close relation to the most striking feature in the apostles' conduct. They always speak and act with authority; they always claim to be armed with the divine power "in the name of Jesus." You can never escape from this claim: the apostles act as wielding superhuman power in virtue of the commission and charge of God. You cannot eliminate this superhuman element from the New Testament; it is implicated in the structure and spirit of every book and every letter. Even though you may reject the book of the Acts—and so get rid of such a punishment as Paul inflicted on Bar-Jesus at Paphos (Acts 13:6–12), you find him claiming to act with the same power at Corinth and at Ephesus. In short, you must either deny the whole, or accept the whole.[6] A nonmiraculous gospel cannot be found by any process of elimination of parts.

Paul claims this superhuman power, not as his own, only as a trust confided to him insofar as the Spirit of God fills him and speaks through him. In estimating its character, we must remember the difference of circumstance between Oriental life and our modern, Western, and northern situation. We must bear in mind the much more impressionable nature of ordinary people in that Levantine world, their susceptibility to demonic influence, the power which climate, sun, sickness, and fever, and many other conditions exercise over them. Much is experienced among them at the present day which would be incredible in our cooler and more self-reliant personalities. Their impressionability produces a far keener physical sympathy, so that one mind can act on another more powerfully. But still, with all these allowances and admissions, you cannot escape the miraculous, superhuman element throughout the New Testament. Power is the keynote throughout; and if you neglect that, you ignore the fundamental fact in the Christian teaching, and inevitably miss its true character.

We need not speculate whether Alexander, who is mentioned here, is identical with "Alexander the coppersmith," who "did me much wrong; the Lord will render to him according to his works" (2 Tim. 4:14). The identity is not impossible, but the word "coppersmith" is more probably added to distinguish this man from the other Alexander who was one of the false teachers.[7] In any case the false teacher, who was a member of the Ephesian church, must be distinguished from Alexander the Jew, evidently not a Christian, who is mentioned in Acts 19:33. The name was extremely common, and was specially favored by Jews in the Greek Hellenic cities. Those who regard it as too strange a coincidence that there should be in the Christian church at Ephesus two persons named Alexander, both of whom opposed Paul, though evidently in different ways, may either identify them, or suppose that the coppersmith belonged to a different town. Timothy was left in charge, not only of Ephesus, but doubtless of all the Asian congregations.

10

The Chief of Sinners

Here, where we regard only historical evidence and treat only historical questions, the religious side of these wonderful words in 1 Timothy 1:16, "sinners, of whom I am chief," does not concern our present purpose. There are no four consecutive words in Paul's writings that throw more light on his character, none which more deserve to be carefully pondered over than these. They have been best understood and most valued by those who have the truest religious feeling. But in this place it is unsuitable and needless to do more than point out what astounding incapacity to understand religious feeling is shown by those who argue that the idea, "sinners, of whom I am chief," is unlike Paul, and can only be the exaggerated imitation of 1 Corinthians 15:9 by some pretender. One is prompted to ask how we can look for sympathetic understanding of Paul's writings from critics to whom the religious feeling is so alien. How can such unsympathetic minds appreciate Paul, or give any illuminating criticism or truthworthy judgment as to what is or is not his work?

One must feel that it is an inconsistent and untenable position to suppose that this letter was written by some person who wished to clothe himself with the authority of Paul in order to acquire more influence in condemning the false teachers of his own later age. And yet that this person, assuming falsely such authority, would make Paul speak of himself as the chief of sinners. How could he think that it would increase the weight of the letter with the Christians of his later age to put such a self-condemnatory phrase in the supposed Paul's mouth? Had he so carefully thought out the imposture as to invent a touch of religious feeling, which has gone direct to the heart of thousands? Who can invent such a wonderful expression of religious emotion except one who feels it in himself? And how can an impostor feel it in his assumed character? And how could the impostor so accurately gauge the character of his readers as to know that they would recognize in this the character of Paul? And was the ordinary Christian of the second century capable of understanding Paul so well as to appreciate this extremely able assumption of his character? That is a series of improbabilities too great for anyone to face.

The only path open to those who deny the Pauline authorship of the Pastoral Epistles is the one which those scholars have as a rule taken, namely, to suppose that the later author who assumed the personality of Paul, while he was ignorantly and irrationally exaggerating and distorting a saying of the great apostle's, blundered into the accidental creation of one of the great religious thoughts—one which has ever since been quoted and cherished by religious minds with grateful hope. It is a necessary accompaniment of this theory that the writer who blundered into the wonderful thought expressed in those words was as blind and insensitive to their religious character as the modern theorists are.

The only other alternative would be to suppose that the unknown forger was by nature and character more Pauline in some of his thoughts than Paul, and that he occasionally penetrated deeper into the mystery of religious emotion than Paul did. But no one is likely ever to maintain or imagine that such a thing is possible. Such a personality would be too powerful to remain hidden in three pseudonymous epistles, and would have influenced his age far too strongly to be forgotten. The modern theorists tacitly reject such a supposition, for they maintain that the later author was consciously imitating and really spoiling a true Pauline saying.

In every direction, the theory of false authorship of these four words breaks down for anyone who can appreciate their religious quality. And literary criticism loses all reason and wanders into a pathless jungle of fancies, unless it proceeds on the principle that a great illuminative or creative saying is to be credited to the author who wrote it as the result of his own genius, and not be reckoned as the result of his blundering exaggeration of some other person's words. What justification is there for applying it to the writer of this epistle? A great thought well expressed must be credited to intention and not to chance error. One may guess at truth, but one does not blunder into truth.

The other class of theorists, who find in the Pastoral Epistles some genuine scraps of Pauline writing mixed up with work by a later hand, might explain 1:16 as a Pauline fragment. But most of them regard it as of later, non-Pauline character, and thus fall under the same condemnation as the advocates of entire forgery.

Knoke, however, has the merit of recognizing this passage of Pauline, though his extraordinarily complicated theory of two different Pauline letters mixed up in scraps with one another and with non-Pauline interpolations will never be accepted by anyone except himself. His analysis is, however, interesting and suggestive.

11

The Object of Prayer
in the Public Assembly

P aul first of all gives some advice about the manner of public worship, not in its entirety, but only in regard to the prayers which should be offered by the congregation. He regards it as a matter of primary importance that the common prayers in the assembly should include the whole human race. There is to be no narrowing of their scope to the church. The benefit of the whole world in which we live, "that all people should be saved and come to the knowledge of the truth" (1 Tim. 2:4), should be prayed for by the saints in every public meeting. The importance attached to this wide charity suggests that some question had arisen as to the scope of Christian prayer. In Ephesians 6:18 prayer "for all the saints" is advised. Here a wider and nobler outlook dictates the instruction.

Now, inasmuch as after Ephesians was written and before this letter to Timothy was composed, there had occurred the terrible events of A.D. 64, when the Christians were treated as monsters and enemies of mankind and the hatred of the Roman mob was roused against them, we can readily understand why Paul now thinks it so important to command that all people should be embraced in the prayers of the congregation. The same fact explains why he immediately adds, "for sovereigns and all that are in high place" (1 Tim. 2:2). You should "pray for them which despitefully use you" (Luke 6:28). There was now great need to emphasize this principle, which the persecution of A.D. 64 might tempt the Christians to forget. Hence a rule is prescribed for this part of the church service, though the other parts of the service are not mentioned, being assumed as sufficiently known and appreciated.

The purpose of the prayers for all the world and for the governing power is that the church may have the peace and tranquility which are favorable to its rapid development and therefore to the ultimate good of all people. The thought is allied to the view taken in 2 Thessalonians 2:1–12 that the imperial power stood between the church and anarchy, protecting it for the time, though destined ultimately to ally itself with the powers of evil against the church.[1] The end was not yet. Peace and order must always be the object of the church's desire and prayers. For the present the emperor was the sovereign, and as such the church prayed for him. The salvation of the world still depended on the continuance of his authority, which was a condition of the preservation of tranquility. Later he should pass away, and a new sovereignty be substituted for him, the sovereignty of the church of God. Von Soden has a note which shows strange misapprehension of this passage, and he has found followers. He thinks that it would be selfish to pray for tranquility, and tries to make out that the tranquil and quiet life is not the object of the church's prayers, but only of Paul's exhortation to pray. In opposition to this opinion, we have attempted to show that a prayer for tranquility was a prayer for the good of all people and for the spread of knowledge of the truth.

12

The Manner and Order of Public Prayer

The bearing of the next verses, 2:8–10, causes difficulty. These words were written with the scene to which they referred clearly pictured before the mind alike of the writer and of his correspondent. It is precisely because they presuppose this perfect acquaintance with the situation in all its details that they are to us obscure and easily open to several interpretations. We have to reproduce before our minds the scene as Paul and Timothy knew it; and if we could do that, then forthwith the words would become clear and their meaning indisputable. But it is difficult for us to reconstruct the scene because the subject is obscure and the evidence extremely scanty.

The critical and decisive question which arises first of all is whether Paul here is thinking of a scene in the assembly where the leader or priest is uttering a prayer and the rest of the congregation is silent, or of a general prayer in which all take part alike. Until that question is answered the interpretation of the passage is involved in confusion and uncertainty. Yet none of the commentators whom I have consulted determines or even proposes the question. Several of them either use ambiguous language which can be understood equally well of common prayer and of prayer uttered by one person on behalf of all, or speak in one sentence as if they held the former view and in another as if they favored the latter. Others definitely take the view that one man prays and the rest keep silence (except, of course, to utter the universal *amen* at the conclusion), apparently without having thought of the other alternative.

When the question is thus fairly and clearly put, it seems hardly possible to avoid the answer that Paul has before his mind a scene of general, common, congregational prayer in which all join equally.

The subject of this common prayer is described in verses 1–2. Then the manner is described in verses 8–9. The balancing against one another of "the men" in verse 8 and of "women" in verse 9 suggests, though certainly it does not definitely prove, that Paul was thinking of an assembly in which the two sexes were not mingled together indiscriminately, but the men stood apart from women. The two groups are conceived as acting "in like manner." This word (ὡσαύτως), coming emphatically as the opening word of the sentence, loses all power and emphasis, and becomes practically meaningless, when the scene is pictured after the fashion in which some commentators understand it, "that the men pray, and that in like manner women dress themselves simply." In fact, this is merely a disjointed collocation of two unconnected ideas, in which the word "in like manner" has no force. The necessary and inevitable sense of this word is that the whole body of women is to be understood as affected by what has been said about the men.

Then Paul, assuming by the word "in like manner" all that has just been said as to prayer, adds further regulations about the conduct and appearance of the women. He was always anxious and troubled about the latter. He felt that the reputation of the church in pagan society, together with the future development of Christian society, depended largely upon them. Both early habit in Tarsus,[1] a thoroughly Oriental city, and reasoned experience during life confirmed his strong opinion that it was unwise and dangerous for Christian women to go far outside of the conventions and current views as to propriety which were accepted in the Greco-Roman world around them. A certain degree of progress was right. The Christian woman then was freer than the Jewish woman. In the Christian congregation women occupied a higher, freer, and more honorable position than they had in Greek society. In the less Hellenized cities of Asia Minor women enjoyed more liberty and influence than in the Greek cities. The early church followed this more liberal and enlightened practice; and the Christian ideal is expressed by the apostle to the Galatians in 3:28: "Christ is the sum of all who believe in him; he takes them all into himself; he admits no distinction of nationality or of rank or of sex; all are placed on an equality and made one in him."[2] This was the ultimate aim and end of Christian society; but to grasp at it prematurely was to sacrifice it. Slavery of men and subjection of women would disappear in the perfect church; but the Christian slave must accept his lot at the moment, and women must act in general accordance with the social ideas of their city and their time.

Paul's advice about women, therefore, always varies between

the ideal and the actual. Early habit made him tend to emphasize the latter side; and ardent feminists will consider that he emphasized it far too much. In this sentence, the phrase "in like manner" expresses something of the ideal, but all the rest is devoted to the emphasizing of the actual and practical conditions. The men should pray with pure hands raised to heaven, and in like manner the women (i.e., should pray). But immediately comes in the thought of the existing social conditions, and the sentence precedes to caution them against too much attention to dress and adornment. In the church assembly, the best way of attaining to the ideal is to attend to the inner character and not to the outer appearance.

Thus both the verbal fact (the use of ὡσαύτως) and the Pauline spirit make us reject the idea that Paul's sole intention here is to assign the duty of praying to the men and to confine the attention of women in church to looking after the character of their dress. Prayer is a part of the church service in which all join.

Paul's advice about public service in every assembly of the congregation (ἐν παντὶ τόπῳ) is confined to the subject and spirit and manner of the common prayer. He has nothing to say about praise or about preaching (except to forbid women absolutely to teach, by which undoubtedly he means public teaching in the assembly [2:12], and certainly does not refer to teaching in the home, which he regarded as a most important element in the development of Christian character [2 Tim. 1:5]). He never mentions the prophesying and other forms of inspired utterance, which indubitably formed an important part of the proceedings in the public assembly. On the other hand in 1 Thessalonians 5:12–20, where he is giving similarly a body of general advice to a young congregation, the only reference which he makes to the duty of assembling in common worship is to utter a caution against depreciating and belittling the inspired utterances of individuals. It would be as absurd to suppose that, when writing to the Thessalonians, Paul had not yet attained to the idea that common prayer should be made in the assembly, as to infer that he now in the epistle to Timothy regards prophesying and ecstatic utterances as unsuitable or unimportant, because he does not allude to them when prescribing rules of conduct for the public assembly. We observe that he never mentions the common meal or the breaking of bread throughout this epistle. Yet no one doubts that, at whatever time the epistle was written, those acts were habitual and most important parts of the congregational life.

The truth is that Paul, who was writing a letter and not a treatise, mentioned only what presented itself to his mind as of urgent consequence. At the moment the custom and order of common prayer was most urgent in the Asian congregations: "first of all I exhort" (where importance, not time, is the principle of order). Doubtless, its importance was as a preventive of the evil that might be caused by false teaching. This regular common prayer was the best means of ensuring "a tranquil and quiet life in all godliness and gravity" under the established law and order of the state, and such a life was exposed to danger from the wild speculation and rash theorizing of the false teachers. Discipline and order were the best safeguard.

Now in this common prayer there was no prescribed form of words. Clement of Rome, in writing to the Corinthians about thirty years later, gives a specimen in his sections 59–61 of what might be said in such prayers, and I cannot doubt that he had in mind this passage of the epistle to Timothy. The words repeated could not be the same, but the thought was to be the same. In such a situation the only method to ensure order and seemliness was that the prayer should be silent; and anyone who has been present at an assembly of the Friends knows how impressive this silent prayer is to all who take part in it. This was known even in the pagan mystic ritual. "One of the most characteristic and significant features in the writings of Ignatius is the emphasis that he lays on silence as something peculiarly sacred and divine. . . . He speaks of God 'who manifested Himself through Jesus Christ His Son, who is His Word that proceeded from silence.'"[3] The silence of the Quakers exacts a high standard of thought.

Such a rule of silent prayer did not exclude the spoken prayer of anyone in the congregation whom the Spirit prompted to pray aloud. That is evident from the whole tone and tendency of the early church. The conclusion from our investigation seems, therefore, to be that in the common prayer there was no official leader who spoke while others listened; it was led only when the Spirit moved a leader. Otherwise it was expressed in common silence and the prayer of thought.

The passage of Clement, which was quoted above, is far from conclusive and definite in its evidence, but on the whole gives the impression of a model for congregational use,[4] not for an individual official taking the lead in prayer. The use of the plural "us" and "we," of course, proves nothing; a single person speaking on behalf of the congregation must use the plural number. But the spirit and tone perceptible in sections 59–61 are subtly different from section 64, which has the evident character of a prayer uttered by an official on behalf of the people. The Jewish usage of that early period, as the Rev. G. H. Box informs me, cannot be determined precisely and certainly. But the custom probably was that, when ten men assembled, they would appoint one of their number to act as the reader. The modern custom is that the Eighteen Benedictions (part of which, especially the first three and the last three, are very early, though the whole series was not fixed in its present form till about A.D. 110) are said first silently by reader and congregation together, and then repeated aloud by the reader.[5] Hence there is great probability that silent prayer of the whole congregation was not unknown in the Jewish synagogues of the first century.

Dr. Sanday, who expresses no definite opinion on either side, points out to me that while in the *Didache* 10.7 the prophets may say as much as they please, the parallel passage in *Apostolic Constitutions* 7 has "presbyters" for "prophets," which would be in favor of ascribing the set form of prayer in *Didache* 10:1–6 to the congregation. It is, as was stated above, part of our view that any inspired person, that is, a prophet or prophetess, might be moved to speak the prayer, while the rest remained silent.

The condition which is prescribed, that the hands of the worshipers be "holy" (ὁσίους), is an interesting point. In the first place, it probably implies that the hands be ceremonially pure, that is, washed immediately before the service begins. This custom of washing before prayer was common both to many pagan cults[6] and to the Jewish ritual. Synagogues and places of prayer (προσευχαί) were commonly placed near running water (Acts 16:13) or beside the sea for the convenience of worshipers. There is very often an artificial fountain of running water within the precinct of a Muslim mosque so that the ablutions may be made easily before entering the sacred building. A fountain or, in places where water was scarce and streams did not exist, a cistern formed a common feature of the sacred precincts that surrounded earlier Anatolian churches;[7] and the Muslim custom (like many of the Muslim tenets) was probably derived from Christian refugees persecuted as heretics by the Orthodox Church. That the Jewish custom should persist in the Pauline congregations of Asia Minor is highly probable. I have elsewhere pointed out examples of the influence of Jewish rites which can be observed in the Anatolian congregations.[8]

In the second place, it would probably be too narrow a view to restrict the force of "holy" hands to ceremonial purity. Although there is always a tendency in human nature to forget the spiritual aspect of a rite and to attend only to the ceremonial and external side, and this tendency worked as strongly in Judaism as in other religions, yet even the Jews in many cases were conscious that external purity was not sufficient without moral purity. Paul was not likely to forget this, nor do the Pastoral Epistles show any signs of neglect in this respect. But it is quite sufficient for us to establish the probability that the external condition of purity was considered and enforced in the earliest Pauline churches of Asia Minor alongside of the moral conditions.

On the other hand, the Jewish analogy, so far as it goes, would favor the view that the men alone prayed in the Pauline church; and would thus be dead against our conjectural restoration of the scene as it was clear in the minds of Paul and Timothy. But we must consider that the early Christian church tended to give greater freedom to women, and that this tendency was restrained by the desire not to offend too distinctly against existing prejudices. Prophetesses might be inspired equally with prophets to speak with tongues and to pray aloud in the assembly; and Paul never forbade this, though he forbade them to give formal teaching or to do anything which assumed a position of authority over men. We may also freely admit that personally he was not favorable to prophetesses speaking publicly at all; but his principle "quench not the Spirit," that is, never belittle or depreciate or discourage any working of the Spirit, would not permit him to forbid them speaking as the Spirit moved them, and he never denied that the Spirit may move women as much as, and in the same way as, he moved men.

13

The Idea of Motherhood
in the Letters of Paul

The apostle is speaking in 1 Timothy 2:9–12 of the conduct of women in the public assembly, though he gradually goes off into the wider topic of their conduct in life generally. They should learn silently (i.e., without asking questions openly in the assembly as men did; cf. 1 Cor. 14:35) in a spirit of peaceful submission to constituted authority (i.e., the officials and the regulations of the church, and also doubtless their husbands),[1] and Paul does not permit them to teach (i.e., publicly in the assembly of the congregation), nor to assume a position of authority over a man, but required them to refrain from (public) action. He is silent about their right to prophesy; but that right he could not deny where the Holy Spirit prompted, though it does not lie in his purpose throughout this letter to emphasize the right of prophesying or speaking with tongues in the assembly either for men or for women.

Then follows a quaint example of the way in which the Jews were wont to derive arguments from Scripture and to twist and torture its words in order to support the opinion which they were stating. Even where Paul is expressing a truth which he sees clearly with direct and unerring intuition, he sometimes draws from the Old Testament arguments which to us seem tortuous special pleading and quite valueless as reasoning. The Jewish mind reasoned in a totally different way from us; and its line of reasoning often offends us. But we must not identify the truth of the opinion with the validity of the reasoning, or conclude that, because the argument is to us unconvincing, the opinion is therefore untrue.

Accordingly, we may set aside as not appealing to our minds and barely intelligible to us the argument drawn from the conduct of Adam and Eve. So far as it is intelligible, it fails to strengthen

Paul's case in the judgment of modern readers. But his case is quite independent of the argument.

Moreover, his argument leads up to a most profound and a much misunderstood remark. In the primordial association with the temptation of evil, woman had been lead into transgression; but the saving power remained in her own nature. What is this saving fact in the nature of woman? Opinion has been much divided as to the meaning of 2:15; and I confess that none of the interpretations which the commentators give seem to touch the real sense and thought of Paul. The leading methods of interpretation are five:

1. She shall be saved through childbearing, that is, as the means of her salvation, a narrow view open to many objections (among others, that it would apparently imply that only a woman who bears a child shall be saved, a thought which is absolutely un-Pauline).

2. She shall be saved during the time of her childbearing. Although that is the period of the curse pronounced on her, yet in it she shall gain salvation, if she continue in faith and love and thanksgiving with sober-mindedness.[2] This interpretation can be defended as an instance of the discursiveness and looseness of the Pastoral Epistles. One feels that it diverges from the direct line of the thought, and that there is about it a want of definiteness and of firm grasp of a central guiding idea. But many will not consider this objection to have any strength, because they find throughout the Pastoral Epistles the same want of that compactness and nervous energy which are characteristic of Paul. But, as it appears to me, the discursiveness of these epistles takes the form of unexpected transition from one thought to another, and of loose connection between the successive ideas and topics that come up for treatment. It rarely appears in any want of definite firm grasp and decisive treatment of each thought singly.

The fault of this interpretation then lies in its being rather weak and disappointing; and those who are not offended by that in the Pastoral Epistles will prefer it. It seems at first sight reasonable and not wholly out of keeping with Paul's tone of mind and thought. Personally I could not accept it; and it may be added that, as regards the language, we should expect that if Paul intended to say this, he would have used the preposition ἐν, not διά. But when one considers this interpretation more carefully, one asks whether it can be Pauline. What does it imply? What is the means through which it supposes that the salvation of the woman is wrought? Through the time of childbearing, in the hour when the primordial curse is upon her, she shall be saved, if she continue in faith and love and thanksgiving with sober-mindedness. Could Paul ever have put salvation on so external an issue as this? Let her be virtuous and she will be saved. One can understand that those who interpret in this fashion cannot accept Paul as the author—unless they have an astonishing power of shutting their eyes and minds to the possibilities of human development in thought. The soul of the Pauline thought lies in the underlying and indwelling idea of power. Where is the power here? There is only a moral platitude.

3. Some scholars therefore abandon wholly the idea that spiritual salvation is involved in the word σωθήσεται, "she shall be saved," because they rightly see that the attempt to import it into the sentence on this construction is a failure. Yet they cling to the construction and take "she shall be saved" in a simpler and purely nonspiritual sense: "Women shall be brought safely through their childbearing, if they continue in faith, etc." The sense is rather poor, narrow, and below the standard of Paul; but those who regard the epistle as a forgery will not see any strength in this objection. But at least they will probably admit that in any work of literature the noblest and widest meaning, if it lies clearly within the unforced words, ought to be credited to the writer; and I think that a much nobler meaning lies within the scope of these words.

4. She shall be saved because of her motherhood, that is, because she is the mother of the race. This sense of διά, "by reason of," can hardly be admitted. Moreover, the course of the thought demands here a statement of the means by which she shall be saved, not of the reason why she shall find salvation.

5. Von Soden, rightly feeling that all these interpretations are poor and unsatisfying, took refuge in a more mystical view. According to him, Paul, when using the term "she" in the singular, is thinking of the generic idea "woman"—which is, of course, quite true—and from this he naturally passes to the idea of the typical woman, Eve. Accordingly woman, that is, all women, shall be saved through the childbearing of the typical woman Eve, because therefrom sprang the Savior Jesus Christ. The thought is extremely ingenious; but it is too clever, and it shipwrecks on the preposition διά, which is takes in the sense "by reason of."

It seems necessary, so far as I can judge, to return to the simple and natural construction, "She shall gain salvation by means of her motherhood (τεκνογονία)." But the whole question turns on what Paul meant when he used this term τεκνογονία. He is thinking philosophically, and not of a mere physical process. We have to take into consideration the whole manner of expression in Greek philosophic thought, and the whole history of Greek progress in language and in thought from the simple and concrete to the philosophic and abstract, from Homer to Aristotle and Paul. In that progress the Greek language was engaged in the creation of abstract nouns, just as Greek thought was teaching itself to generalize and to distinguish between ideas which are bound up with one another in the concrete world. If we had before us the works of Athenodorus the Tarsian, we should be better able to appreciate the linguistic task which Paul had to perform when he sought to express in Greek a Christian philosophy, and better able to understand the way in which he attempted to solve the problem before him.[3]

We must remember how *simple* and *concrete* are often the terms by which Greek attempted to express the highest thoughts of moral and metaphysical philosophy. Plato hardly attempted to create a language of the higher philosophy. He argues in the concrete example; he takes refuge in metaphor and poetry and myth when he must attempt to give expression to the highest philosophical ideas. Aristotle set himself to create a technical terminology in the region of metaphysics, and how simple are his means. The essential nature of a thing is "the what-is-it?" of the thing, τὸ τί ἐστι, that is, "the answer to the question, what is it?" The idealized goodness of a thing is τό ἀγαθῷ εἶναι; the law of its development is to τὸ τί ἦν εἶναι.[4] How perfectly plain and common are the words! How close to ordinary life! And yet what a lofty philosophic sense does Aristotle read into them.

Or again, let us turn to the Attic tragedy, which sounded the depths and estimated the heights of human feeling. I take an example which leads up suitably to the thought in this passage of the Tarsian apostle—a passage the discussion of which by a modern writer[5] first opened to me the realm of Greek thought, and showed me, when I was a student in Aberdeen, how different is interpretation from translation, and how easily one may learn to translate without having any conception of the real meaning of an ancient poet. Sophocles in the *Electra* pictures Clytemnestra as she realizes the dread bond of emotion that unites a mother to her son. She appreciates its power all the better that it is unwelcome to her. It is too strong for her, and masters her will. And how does she express this? She uses no abstract terms, but four of the simplest and most commonplace words, δεινὸν τὸ τίκτειν ἐστίν. Those who are content with translating according to the lexicon would render these words, "the giving birth to a child is a painful thing," and miss all the wealth of feeling and thought that lies in them. There cannot be a doubt that Sophocles was expressing the truth,[6] which everyone must appreciate who passes through the real experiences of life, that there is no power in human nature more tremendous, more overmastering, more dreadful to contemplate in some of its manifestations, than the tie of motherhood. Only when the human nature in her is deadened and brutalized or buried, can the woman become stronger than that tie. It is the divine strength moving in her, and it can bend or break her if she resists.

In this feeling of motherhood Paul found the power that he needed for his purpose. Here is the divine strength in the nature of woman, which can drive her as it will and which will be her salvation, "if she continue in faith and love and thanksgiving with sobermindedness," but which may drive her in the wrong direction if it be not guided by those qualities. The idea of power, of growth, of striving towards an end outside of oneself, always underlies Paul's conception of the relation of a human being towards God. To his Greek hearers he often compared the true Christian life to the straining effort of a runner competing for the prize, because he knew that there he touched a feeling which was extraordinarily strong in the mind of a Greek man. In the woman's nature the maternal instinct presented itself as a force that had more absolute power over her than any emotion in a man's nature had over him. Paul rarely touches on the love between the sexes, and had small respect for it as a divine emotion capable under proper guidance of working out the salvation of either man or woman.

In giving expression to this psychological observation, Paul was under the influence of his own time, when philosophical expression was more developed. Abstract nouns had been created in great numbers to express the higher ideas of thought; an abstract noun was needed to express this idea of the power of maternal instinct. And Paul found it in τεκνογονία, which is a simpler and certainly not a less reasonable or correct term than a sham word like "philoprogenitiveness" or a question-begging circumlocution like "maternal instinct."

Thus, as so often elsewhere in the Pastoral Epistles, the apparent difficulty is caused by a wrong point of view, and disappears as soon as one looks from the right point of view. The maternal instinct does not require actual physical motherhood. It may be immensely powerful in a childless woman and may be her salvation, though it is, of course, quickened in a wonderful degree towards her own child, and is often dormant until so quickened.

I do not remember that Paul touches this spring of life in any of his earlier letters. But what rational critic would find in that any proof that this letter is not his composition? Is there any of Paul's letters which does not throw its own distinct rays of light on his character? Is there any of them which can be cut away without narrowing and impoverishing to some degree our knowledge of his nature? Must we regard it as an essential condition in proving the genuineness of the Pastoral Epistles that they should contain nothing which widens our knowledge of him or throws new light on his character? Rather, would it now be a conclusive reason against Pauline authorship, if it were wholly immaterial to our conception of Paul's personality whether they were accepted or rejected? Moreover, we observe also that, in writing to Timothy, Paul addressed one who probably gained from his home life a strong sense of what maternal feeling is. Paul had a marvelous power of unconsciously sympathizing with his correspondents. It is only in writing to Timothy that he gives a picture of home life (2 Tim. 1:5) under a mother's care. He uses the word "mother" twice in writing to Timothy. Except in two quotations from the Old Testament (Eph. 5:31, 6:2), he uses it only three times in all the rest of his letters put together—Romans 16:13 as a metaphor to express his affection for a friend's mother[7] and Galatians 1:15; 4:26 in a generic and unemotional sense. He does not show the want of love for the idea of mother which is conspicuous in Horace;[8] but except in sympathy with Timothy he nowhere shows a deep sense of what a mother is and feels and does to her child.

These considerations explain why two words otherwise unknown in Paul's writings[9] are forced on him in expressing his thought on this subject. The word for grandmother is "un-Pauline," but where else could Paul use it except in 2 Timothy 1:5? Where else does his interest in family life appear? The word for motherhood is used only in 1 Timothy 2:15, but that is the only place in which he speaks of the idea that lies in the word. The wider terminology of the Pastoral Epistles, called through a too narrow outlook "un-Pauline," really corresponds to and is the inevitable result of a wider range of thought.

The use of the verb τεκνογονεῖν in the physical sense in 1 Timothy 5:14 is no proof that the abstract noun derived from it must also have the physical sense in Paul. Sophocles uses τίκτειν often in the physical sense, but that does not prevent him from employing it in the philosophic or emotional sense in the passage quoted above.

14

The Bishops or Elders
of the Congregation

The description of the character of bishops and deacons (1 Tim. 3:1–7) is probably largely responsible for the prejudice against the Pastoral Epistles; and it cannot be denied that there is a certain externality about the passage. Nowhere else does Paul in so long a passage say so little that touches the heart of his subject or of humankind. Here again the difficulty seems to lie in the point of view. The opinion seems to be commonly entertained—to judge from much of what has been written on these passages—that Paul is describing the ideal bishop and the ideal deacon. Nothing can be further from the truth.

What then was the writer's intention in those words, and how did he understand that Timothy should read them? As it appears to me, Paul indicates in the opening words the intention which he has, and the point of view from which the whole passage must be understood by the reader. "If a man desires the office of bishop, he is seeking for an honorable work."[1] This statement, put so prominently at the beginning of the paragraph, is extremely important. The question then is what we are to gather from the opening sentence, on which Paul evidently lays so strong emphasis.

In the first place, this statement implies that the office was aimed at and sought for: in other words, there were candidates for the office, persons who were known to be desirous of the office. This is not consistent with the opinion that bishops were selected and appointed by one single administrator or head. In the church of that period, where the Holy Spirit was the inspiring and guiding influence, there can be no doubt that any single head of the church, such as Paul himself in some cases or as Timothy at Ephesus in the present case, would act under the guidance of the Holy Spirit and pick out and appoint on his own responsibility and of his own knowledge, with or without consultation, "as seemed good to the Holy Spirit and to him." He would not call for candidates, and would make his selection among those who applied for the office. He would know well that the best man might not apply at all. Paul, in these words, anticipates and approves of candidature; and therefore he does not understand that Timothy was to nominate the bishops. The only alternative is that the congregation, either directly or through its offices and representatives, made the appointment by some form of election out of those who were candidates.

In the second place, it follows from this that the rest of the passage describing the bishop is to be understood as advice about the scrutiny of candidates. Paul is not describing the ideal. Had he been doing that he would not have exhausted himself in a long list of qualities, but rather would have set before us a living being. He is dealing with the practical difficulty of sorting out and estimating the candidates. The electors may suitably begin by scrutinizing them, and setting aside those who are deficient in any of the qualifications which a bishop ought to have. But a bishop should have more than mere qualifications. Doubtless Paul held that he must be inspired by the Holy Spirit; but at present he is only concerned with the practical difficulty of the preliminaries to appointment or election.

In the third place, we observe that in the parallel passage Titus 1:5–9, there is no allusion to candidates. Titus has to discharge forthwith the difficult duty of appointing elders in all the cities. It was the same task which Paul had to perform when he returned through all the cities of Galatia (Acts 14: 21–23), because his sudden expulsion during his first visit had prevented the proper organization of the several churches. This was a different task from what lay before Timothy in the cities of Asia. The whole body of officials had to be quickly appointed in the Cretan cities; the whole organization had to be created. Each congregation had to be scrutinized man by man, each individual's claims and merits to be estimated, and his faults considered. Paul sketches out the way in which Titus may set about this task: probably election played some part even in Crete, but much influence would be exercised by Titus in consultation with those whom he knew to be leading men in the congregation.

In the Asian cities, among which Timothy was stationed, the churches had been long established and organized. The attainment of office in the commonwealth of God was an object of desire, and Paul approves of this desire. But he recognizes also that when an office rouses desire, it may become an object of ambition and may be sought for the sake of distinction, not for the sincere purpose of performing the onerous work attached to it. Hence, while expressing approval of the desire, he also states that it is a work (not a mere honor)[2]; and he enumerates the qualifications that are required to do the work.

In the fourth place, the remarks in our preceding paragraph have made it clear that the whole passage about the bishops is not merely advice to Timothy and to other electors. It is also a caution to candidates, that they may examine themselves before publicly professing their aspiration. This is one of the cases in which the letter, though primarily a letter to Timothy personally, was influenced by the thought of reaching others.

Apart from general moral qualities which are universal conditions of church membership, there are certain qualifications that attract notice. The bishop must be "given to hospitality." It has often been noted[3] how important a part in the early church was played by frequent intercourse between the scattered congregations. That was essential to its existence: without that its cohesion as an institution and its unity in belief and practice could not have been maintained. Traveling was, therefore, frequent among the Christians; and the experience of finding everywhere amid the alien pagan society bands of fellow Christians thinking and believing alike had a powerful influence on the traveler, as we know from the epitaph which the early Phrygian saint, Avircius Marcellus, wrote in his old age to be placed over his own grave.[4] An important duty for all the brethren, and especially for the officials and representatives, was that they should be "given to hospitality." Their brother from a distant land must not be let out of their home life to find a dwelling for himself during his stay. He must be welcomed and must live among the brethren. Nor need it be thought that this hospitality was shown only to fellow Christians. It was certainly shown also to the poor and needy and sick, whatever their religion. This procedure increased the influence of the church, strengthened its position in society, and offered many opportunities for proselytizing. The public inns were usually filthy and immoral;[5] and were avoided as much as possible by all travelers. Guest-friendship for mutual hospitality was common, and was reckoned among the pagans as a strong bond of union; nor was the force of this tie likely to be neglected by the Christians in their relations to the pagan society around them.

The bishop is required to be "apt to teach." Considering how much Paul's mind was occupied with the dangers caused in Ephesus by the false teachers, we cannot doubt that this requirement has the effect of laying on the bishop the responsibility of correcting the false teaching by imparting the true teaching. That this is so appears from Titus 1:9, where the requirement is more fully expressed. When he was writing to Timothy, Paul had in the earlier part of his letter expressed his opinion emphatically and fully about false and true teaching, and he therefore had no need to explain what he had in mind as to the bishop's teaching. But in writing to Titus, he had not alluded to the subject previously, and therefore it was needful to specify definitely what the bishops had to teach, and that they must know how to supply the antidote to the false teaching. Accordingly, instead of the single word διδακτικός "apt to teach," Paul, though he was aiming at brevity much more than in 1 Timothy, substituted the elaborate statement, "holding to the faithful word which is according to the teaching, that he may be able both to exhort in the sound doctrine, and to convict the gainsayers." That was all implied in the single word "apt to teach," as Paul used it. In this we have a good example of the creativeness of Paul in language, and of the manner in which the needs of the situation caused the creation of the new terms which abound in the Pastoral Epistles.[6] Not that the Greek adjective was coined by Paul. It is so obvious and natural a formation that it was doubtless used already by other philosophic writers, and it occurs in Philo. But Paul gave it a new and far richer meaning than it had before. He wanted to sum up in one word the requirement which was so much in his mind at the time, and he seized on this word and used it in the sense of "qualified by education and moral power to impart the sound Christian teaching in opposition to the many false teachers." He had never used the word before because he had never needed it. The new circumstances demanded a word, and he supplied it.

We have here also a good example of the manner in which several slight differences between the two descriptions of the bishop, similar in thought and word as they are, were necessitated by the different circumstances of Timothy and Titus. Another example has been given above in regard to the appointment of the bishops. A third will be stated in an immediately following page.

Such slight variations to suit difference of situation prove that we have before us two original letters adapted to two real occasions by one writer, and not two forged epistles concocted in imaginary circumstances, addressed to two names taken out of ancient history, but intended to emphasize one thought in one crisis of the church. The two letters have the living quality of adaptation to real situations similar and yet different from one another.

It may seem at first sight strange to us that Paul should think it needful to state the requirement that the bishop should not be given to wine-drinking,[7] and should not be the sort of person that strikes others with his fists: two faults which naturally go together in a rude class of society. But we have always to bear in mind that Paul is speaking about congregations where all (except a few Jews) were converts from paganism, many of them very recent converts; and that such new brethren could not always be trusted not to relapse into their old ways and faults of life. Hence Paul requires that the bishop must not be a recent convert, but one who had been a Christian long enough to have proved his steadfastness and the consistency and certainty of his standard in living. He knew well (and his knowledge finds brief expression in verse 6) that the novice, converted in a moment of exalted feeling, often proved unable to maintain his life continuously on the same high level. Paul had learned by many bitter lessons that the novices had to be watched over,[8] and that some of them, especially if they were blinded with self-conceit about the high standard of life to which they had attained, were liable to make a terrible breakdown and fall under the jeering condemnation pronounced by the enemy of all good (a term which includes not merely the devil as the archenemy, but all who gird at the good man and triumph when he falls into misconduct). This allusion to wine-drinking and fighting brings out very clearly that Paul in this list is (as was said above) not describing the ideal bishop, but showing how to weed out the list of candidates.

Another of the differences between the Cretan and the Asian churches appears in the prohibition against admitting novices to be candidates for a position among the bishops. In the corresponding passage of the letter to Titus novices are not alluded to. Titus had to select the elders or bishops in new congregations where all were novices; he must do his best with such material as he had. On the other hand, Ephesus and many Asian cities contained congregations which had by the time existed for a considerable period, and here there was a patent distinction between new converts and those of longer standing.

We observe also that the term novice, or new convert, could hardly occur in Paul's earlier writings, but only in his last letters. A certain time must pass before the founder can write to the churches which he himself has founded in terms which presuppose a recognized distinction between new and old members. Could such a distinction by any possibility have existed in Galatia when Paul wrote to the Galatians? Or in Asia when he wrote to the Ephesians and Colossians? The nearest approach to such a possibility was in

Philippi, when the epistle to that city was written; but even there distinctly less time had passed over the church than in Ephesus when Paul wrote to Timothy. And even assuming that the distinction was recognized in Philippi when Paul was writing, he did not exhaust his vocabulary in the one short letter to the Philippians. Moreover, the growth of such a distinction and of a word (or words rather) to express it could take place only when the churches of Aegean lands were as a body beginning to attain some age and standing. The idea in the word is thoroughly Pauline. Paul uses φυτεύειν ("to plant") to indicate conversion; and when he wanted a word to indicate new converts, it was natural that he should employ the term νεόφυτος ("newly planted"). One could not easily find in any writer a better example of the growth of his vocabulary, proceeding within his own mind through the widening of his experiences, and based on his older vocabulary, than in this growth of the later Pauline νεόφυτος out of the older Pauline φυτεύειν.

The distinction between novices and Christians of longer standing and experience implied that two terms would grow up to express the two classes. How would Paul have described the older class? Would he have used the periphrasis ἀρχαῖος μαθητής (Acts 21:16), by which Luke designated Mnason? At any rate, the term used by Luke indicates that the distinction of the two classes was beginning to be felt in the church generally during the lifetime of Luke, and we shall find it hard to draw any strong line between Luke and Paul.

The reference to the opinion entertained in pagan society about the bishop is interesting. It was Paul's practice, as we see in the case of Timothy, to take account of the reputation which one whom he was thinking of placing in a position of authority or responsibility had gained among the brethren. But it may seem strange that here the testimony of the brethren should not be alluded to,[9] whereas good reputation among the pagans is a condition which should be applied in scrutinizing the candidates for the office of bishop. The opinion of the brethren, however, cannot here be a condition because it constitutes the method of election; and it would be mere verbiage to say that a person who is to be appointed by vote of the brethren must have their good opinion. As the church was surrounded by critical pagan society, the election of one who was considered by the pagans not to be a worthy and good man would be a dangerous thing. The tongue of scandal and reproach would be let loose against him and against the congregation amid which he had been placed in authority. Thus he would fall into the snare which the devil is always laying for all Christians.

It is evident that this condition, which is stated last by a sort of afterthought, merely repeats and enlarges the condition which is placed first of all, that the bishop must be free from reproach. In the corresponding passage in the letter to Titus, the first condition is stated twice, as it is here. But the second statement gives precision to it in a different fashion: a bishop, as being the steward of God, must be subject to no imputation. The two passages are in this point parallel to one another. Both place this condition in the forefront, as of the highest importance; both repeat it a second time, making it more definite. There may very well have been in the varying forms of the repetition some special suitability to the respective cases of Ephesus and Crete; but we have not sufficient information to judge on this point.

The conditions which are to be applied in choosing bishops and deacons, as stated to Titus, do not otherwise vary essentially from those stated to Timothy. The terms selected to describe the moral qualities vary without any noteworthy divergence in moral character. It is remarkable that in each passage Paul uses some words which he never employs except in these two epistles, and that also (where they differ) he uses some which he never employs except in the single epistle. That again illustrates the origin of Paul's new language in the Pastorals. In none of Paul's other letters have we any list of this kind. New terms were necessary, and yet Paul does not confine himself to one set of new terms, but draws from his great store of language with inexhaustible profusion, so that in stating what is practically the same list twice over, he uses two different sets of novel words.

At the same time both the contrast between novices and old converts, and the growth of new words to express new ideas and conditions in the church imply a distinct interval dividing the Pastoral from the other epistles of Paul. They are not intelligible as contemporary with the others, but only in succession to them.

15

Qualifications of the Deacons

The rules (or rather the advice, for there is no real question of fixed regulations in the letters) about deacons are very similar in character to those about bishops or elders. Corresponding to the lesser importance of the office, they are more briefly given. But it would be a mistake to conclude too quickly that the differences are due solely to abbreviation or omission of some of the principles respecting the bishops. The variations require to be examined in detail and are not uninstructive. We are deprived of the help of comparison with the other Pastorals, as deacons are not mentioned in Titus, and in 2 Timothy 4:5 the diaconate of Timothy is merely spoken about in general terms (translated "ministry" in the NIV and NRSV).

It would at first sight appear as if the condition of good reputation required for the bishops, and regarded in their case as so important that their reputation even among the pagans must be scrutinized, was not required in the selection of deacons. But instead of it a much more effective provision is introduced, which attains the desired end in a more certain way: there shall be a certain period or kind of probation before they are definitely appointed: "but let these also first be proved; then let them serve as deacons, if they be blameless" (1 Tim. 3:10).

In Meyer-Weiss's *Kommentar* it is maintained that the opening phrase, καὶ οὗτοι δέ, indicates "the deacons in distinction from the bishops;" and yet in the same work it is maintained that the "proving" of the deacons is substantially the same process as the examination of the reputation of the bishops. But there is no need for the adversative "but" if the process is the same in both cases. Meyer-Weiss put forward as a reason for the adversative that in the case of the bishops only those qualifications are mentioned which can be observed through scrutiny of their past life, whereas in the case of deacons regard is paid also, and especially, to those qualifications whose presence will first be shown in the exercise of the duties of their office. Surely, however, it is as important to scrutinize the latter class of qualities in a bishop as in a deacon. Moreover, when Meyer-Weiss give examples of the latter class of qualities, they mention only two: "not given to much wine," and "not greedy of filthy lucre." Now with regard to those two qualities we observe that (1) they are expected and mentioned also in the case of a bishop[1] and (2) it is simply absurd and pure verbiage to say that those qualities could be detected only in the discharge of a deacon's office and not earlier. There is no quality easier to detect and more difficult to hide than the tendency to drink; and there is very little, if any, reason to think that in the circumstances of ancient life the deacon would be more exposed to temptation in this respect after than before he took office.

Even if we assume that Meyer-Weiss are right, and that the peculiar form of this provision in the case of deacons is intended to ensure qualities which can be observed only in the actual discharge of their duties, the best way would be to submit the deacons to a probation as well as to a scrutiny of their past life. But Meyer-Weiss will not admit that a probation (in the full sense which is ordinarily attached to the word) was intended. It must, of course, be allowed that the Greek word[2] does not necessarily imply probation, and is quite well satisfied by a careful scrutiny; but Meyer-Weiss lay special emphasis on the fact that exactly the same kind of scrutiny was applied to the bishops.[3]

For my own part I cannot understand the pointed contrast expressed between the testing of deacons and that of bishops except on the supposition that there was some distinct difference in the two cases; and the most natural and probable supposition seems to be that a deacon had to go through some kind of probation, whereas a bishop was elected and appointed forthwith. Such was the view taken by Luther and others of Paul's intention in these words.[4]

That a deacon should undergo probation, from which a bishop was exempt, evidently arises from the fact that no bishops were chosen who had not already abundantly proved their character in the eyes of all the world, whereas younger and less known persons were often appointed as deacons. Hence, even at Ephesus no condition is made by Paul that the deacon must not be "a novice" (v. 6): on the other hand, he evidently contemplated the possibility that neophytes might be chosen as deacons.

Thus, in examining the difference in respect of the tests imposed on the elders and the deacons, we have incidentally found the reason why a difference exists in the condition as to length of Christian experience in the two cases.

As to the condition that the deacon must be grave (σεμνός; v. 8), while the bishop must be temperate, sober-minded, orderly (νηφάλιος, σώφρων, κόσμιος; v. 2), these seem to be mere varieties of expression. The Greek word σεμνό is defined very well by the other three adjectives. In respect of those purely moral qualities we observed in the preceding section that considerable difference of language (but little of real meaning) existed in the conditions for selection of a bishop in Titus, from those which are mentioned in 1 Timothy.

A much more important variation is found in the very first remark made about the bishop, that "if a man seeks after the office of a bishop, he desires an honorable work" (v. 1). Nothing exactly similar is said in respect of a deacon. We inferred that Paul emphatically expressed his approval of candidature for the position of a presbyter or bishop. Did he, then, not desire to encourage Christians to seek after the office of deacon? The question suggests at once the answer. He encourages people to do so at the end of his regulations, but expresses himself in a different way: "They that have served well as deacons gain to themselves a good standing, and great boldness in the faith" (v. 13). This corresponds to the encouragement given to bishops, and the variation is suited to the difference of duties. There can hardly be a doubt, and, so far as I have observed, no one expresses any doubt that Paul's words imply that a good deacon would have an improved chance of being elected to the office of bishop, because he becomes better known and more valued for the qualities that he possesses.

This does not imply that the diaconate was a lower and the bishopric a higher grade in a fixed order of ministry. But it is clear that the duties and the position of a deacon were humbler in character than those of a bishop. But in actual life, and especially under the Roman Empire, where the idea of gradation of service and of promoting from lower to higher office in a fixed order was familiar to all, there was a strong and inevitable tendency to make the diaconate a stage preliminary to the bishopric, though there was no such implication in Paul's words. The idea of gradation came in and governed the common practice in the church; but the Pauline freedom was not lost for many centuries, and occasional examples occurred in which bishops were appointed who had not gone through the lower grade.

There is also a difference of language in regard to another condition. The bishop must be "apt to teach" (διδακτικός; v. 2). This was an important side of his duty, and his qualifications for it must be evident before his appointment. That the deacon should have proved himself apt to teach is not required; but this does not mean that teaching was outside of his sphere of duty. All Christians should be teachers (as Paul held in unison with the spirit of the entire church); and *a fortiori* a deacon should teach. But it is not required that he should have shown special aptitude (as it is in the case of a bishop). It is required only that he should have the fundamental quality of true faith and knowledge, "holding the mystery of the faith in a pure conscience" (v. 9). He may have this mystery hidden deep in his heart and lack the power of setting it in words before others; but he must have the mystery in his heart. In his life as a deacon he will acquire experience in making it known to others, and thus "gain to himself great boldness in the faith which is in Jesus Christ" (v. 13). The last consideration places it beyond doubt that the deaconship was understood by Paul as a good preparation for the office of bishop, though not as a necessary preliminary stage in the progress towards it.

There remain two other points of difference in the qualifications of deacons and presbyters, which are noteworthy as throwing some light on the duties of the two offices. The bishop must be given to hospitality; no such qualification is required for the deacon. It has been often pointed out that the bishop was the representative of the congregation both in its relations with other congregations and in its relations with the pagan world generally and the state. Hospitality was a duty incumbent on bishops beyond others, though of course it was a duty for all Christians. The bishops, however, were responsible for this, and specially charged with the entertainment of delegates from and the communication by letter with other congregations. It would be difficult for a bishop to exercise this hospitality without a certain command of money; and hence various consequences spring from it, which need not here be discussed. As the representative of the congregation in its relations with the pagan world, the city authorities and the imperial government, it would be specially needful that the bishop should "have good testimony from them that are without" (v. 7).[5]

The deacon had no special need for this qualification. He was not responsible for hospitality, except in the same way as all Christians were. He did not represent the congregation in the eyes of the outer world.

On the other hand, the deacon must not be "double-tongued" (δίλογος; v. 8). Nothing similar is said in regard to the bishops. It might be suggested that this was implied in the other moral qualities with which he must be endowed. But stress is laid on it in the case of the deacon (who, as we saw, is required to have a similarly high character); and therefore, it must have been a quality peculiarly needed in his case, that is, he must in his duties have been under strong temptation to become "double-tongued." The word implied a person who spoke sometimes in one fashion, sometimes in another, who would say one thing to one person and another thing to another. Now there can be no doubt that the work of deacons was more closely connected with the indoor and family life of members of the congregation than the work of presbyters. The deacons had more intimate duties in the administration of charity and help where it was needed. They had to find out the needs of individuals, to go about among the members of the congregation, and to converse and to sympathize with them. There was great temptation to say too much to one person or in one family, and thus to be betrayed into inconsistency and self-contradiction in speaking to another. Nothing is easier than for a person to slip into the fault of double-tonguedness when he is trying to accommodate himself to various families in one congregation. Sound sense and perfect straightforwardness are the safeguard; and those qualities were not useless in a deacon.

The minute examination of the conditions prescribed in the selection of deacons affords a strong presumption that the first epistle to Timothy is a real letter written in the stress of practical administration by an administrator familiar with the situation. The conditions are so detailed and minute, and the variations from the conditions prescribed for the bishops are so slight and yet so suitable, that one cannot imagine how a writer who was (according to the now fashionable view) piecing together scraps of letters written by Paul and adding parts to connect these scraps after a fashion, could produce such a result. From a process like that there could never come forth a letter which reflects so accurately the facts of practical life. Equally impossible is it to suppose that a writer of the second century, whose object was to use the authority of Paul's name against a current heresy, could work in so much minute positive regulation into his polemic, which was in intention negative.

16

Deaconesses

In the middle of the regulations about deacons there is interposed a short statement about women: "After the same fashion women must be grave, not scandal-mongers, temperate, faithful in all things" (1 Tim. 3:11). Then the discussion of deacons proceeds.

From the situation of this sentence and from the introductory word "in like manner" (ὡσαύτως), it seems beyond question that this sentence refers not to Christian women in general, but to the class of women who were selected for congregational work, that is, deaconesses. The word *diakonos* is understood generically of both sexes, without actually using the official title *diakonissa*. This was facilitated by the fact that the deaconesses were sometimes called by the same form in Greek διάκονοι (and Paul himself speaks in that way [Rom 16:1]).

As to the qualifications of women officials in the church, the reasons are obvious. Their work was in the home life of the congregation. They had to mix with the Christian families, and to be intimately acquainted with domestic circumstances. There is appropriateness in the provision that they must be specially free from any tendency to talk in one house about the affairs of another; that tendency is almost inseparable from the spreading of slander (μὴ διάβολοι). The analogy to the provision about deacons (μὴ δίλογοι; v. 8) is evident, and the reason is similar. That they should be characterized by self-command and by trustworthiness in every respect is obvious.

It has been thought by Luther and others (e.g., Von Soden) that the women who are here meant are the wives of deacons. There can, however, be little, if any, doubt, that the reference is to all women officially selected for congregational work. But the question is an open one, whether the wives of deacons may not have been chosen by preference as deaconesses. The question has been raised in reference to some Lycaonian Christian inscriptions of the fourth century; but the evidence was found insufficient to justify any positive conclusion.[1] Some of the inscriptions suggest the thought that the wives of deacons and presbyters may perhaps have borne the title of their husbands. There was among the pagans a tendency, and even in some cults a positive custom, that the wife of a priest was officially a priestess; and it is quite likely that among the Christians some tendency to appoint husband and wife as deacon and deaconess prevailed.

17

Were the Officials a Clerical Order?

D r. Plummer, in his excellent work on the Pastoral Epistles,
regards it as one of the four or five fundamental inferences
from which his investigation starts, that in 1 Timothy and the other
Pastoral Epistles there is implied a distinction already clear and
recognized between an order of clergy and the ordinary members
of the congregation, the laity.[1]

It may be questioned whether this does not introduce a later
thought and a later classification. Probably we have in the Pastorals
only an older form of thought and organization which developed
later into this distinction.

It is quite evident that there existed in Paul's mind, and in the
actual facts of the situation in the early churches, a strong and well-
marked distinction between officials and the ordinary members of
the congregation. But it does not seem to the present writer so clear
as it does to Dr. Plummer that this distinction was exactly similar
to what is understood in modern times as the distinction between
clergy and laity. The official was one of the ordinary congregation
selected for a special purpose, in order that he might devote himself
continuously to a certain series of duties; but it does not appear
that those duties lay outside of the sphere of any ordinary Christian.
On the contrary, it appears rather that those duties were incumbent
on all Christians, although in the circumstances of life it was difficult
or impossible for most people to give continuous or sufficient
attention to them. The duties had to be performed in order that the
congregation might preserve its unity and be an organic body; but
all members of the congregation were equally eligible as officials
according to their fitness. At any moment any member might be
selected by the voice and consent of his fellows for official position
and honor; and such general consent and opinion was apparently
regarded as the inspiration of the Holy Spirit. Any such spontaneous

yet solemn act of choice would have been naturally and reverently expressed in the words of the decree issued by the apostolic congress in Jerusalem (Acts 15:28): "It seemed good to the Holy Spirit and to us."

Does this amount to the distinction between the clergy and the laity, as it is now understood? Certainly it shows an essential difference from the distinction as it is understood in the Roman Catholic Church. The bishop is to Paul an ordinary good Christian householder, ruling his family well. It is not to be understood that he *must* have a family; but that certainly was no disqualification (as it is in the modern Roman Catholic Church). And one cannot but feel that Paul, having regard to actual facts in a congregation and to human nature, had acquired the conviction that it was a positive recommendation in a candidate for office, that he had shown himself a judicious head of a family. The number of those who could lead the divine life devoted to God and sacrificing the family relationship (1 Cor. 7:7ff.) was too small to keep the congregational organization in good working order. Those exceptional persons would display their special fitness when they arose; but these recommendations are intended to guide choice among the ordinary church members and take no account of exceptional cases, which will impose themselves by their own power and the power of the Spirit.

No preparation or special training is prescribed either for bishops or deacons. The nearest approach to a period of training is the probation (whatever that was) which was prescribed in the selection of deacons. When an order of clergy comes into existence, a period and system of training, instruction, and preparation becomes practically a necessity. Every Christian was potentially a priest, though circumstances might deny him the opportunity of developing his position and training to its proper consummation. With such a view it seems inconsistent to draw any deep or essential distinction between priest and laity after the modern fashion (if I rightly understand that fashion).

Was the office of deacon or of bishop understood by Paul as one that could be laid down at will? Could the bishop sink back into the position of an ordinary member of the congregation? It is certain that the office was permanent and not for a stated period. It was not on the level of the magistracies in the Hellenic cities, to which one was elected for a year or even less. It was on the grade of certain offices, chiefly or entirely hieratic, in the cities of Asia, which were held for life (διὰ βίου). The individual was chosen on account of his fitness, and his fitness was practically a permanent and inalienable characteristic. There is in these regulations no question of or opening for relapse from the higher position.

Whether degradation in case of proved unfitness was possible is not stated. Paul's intention is to guard against the need of degradation by care in selection. He is not formulating a code of laws to meet all possible emergencies, but giving advice as to the best way of performing the urgent and unavoidable duty of selecting bishops and deacons.

That the office carried with it higher rank in the congregation is evident throughout. Office is a worthy object of desire. Christians should aim at office, and are encouraged to be candidates for office. There is no reason to think that the number of officials was fixed so that choice was needed only when a vacancy occurred. On the contrary, the clear assumption throughout is that no one is chosen unless he possesses the qualifications entirely and without drawback. There is no question of filling up a vacancy by choosing the best available person, even though he has not all the qualifications. The Christian ideal is different. Everyone who is fully worthy is chosen. It is not a case where a crown is awarded only to the single best competitor; all who deserve it win it. The position of bishop or of deacon is honorable; but it means a life of continuous, self-sacrificing work, not of mere outward honor and display.

The question, therefore, whether the officials in the Pauline churches formed a clerical order as distinguished from the laity becomes a question of definition. What is meant by the terms clergy and laity? As those terms are now commonly understood, there was no such distinction in the early congregations. But there was a clear distinction between officials and ordinary members. The officials had proved to general opinion their right to be officials, that is, to do habitually all that a Christian should do, and to be trusted with the management of the business and corporate life of the whole body. And that business was mainly, but not entirely, religious and charitable, didactic and hospitable; the officer was the servant of the servants of God.

If the definition of a clerical order is simply that the members have been marked out by the "laying on of hands," and if all other characteristics and conditions are regarded as unimportant, then there was a clerical order in the early Pauline churches; but it was very different institution from the clergy in the modern churches.

The meaning of the bishop's and deacon's qualification, that he must be "no lover of money" (1 Tim. 3:3) or "not greedy of filthy lucre" (3:8), has perhaps some bearing on this question. The general understanding seems to be that this indicates simply superiority to bribery. This is, no doubt, included in the connotation of the two terms; and that common Oriental failing was at least as dangerous and as necessary to guard against in the Eastern church as it would be in the West. But one may well doubt whether that was the chief thought in Paul's mind. The second term, which is used about both bishops and deacons, means rather "not gaining money by dishonorable means," and really points to the idea that an official must not be engaged in any disgraceful or low-class trade. The thought is specially a Roman one. In Rome certain trades, which were reckoned dishonorable such as that of an auctioneer, constituted a disqualification legally for public office. Paul, having in the first place used the more general term, "not a lover of money" (ἀφιλάργυρος), afterwards employed the more definite expression (μὴ αἰσχροκερδής).

This raises the further question whether the bishop, on election to office, abandoned his trade, and devoted himself wholly to official duties. That is a question which has been elsewhere treated; but there seems every probability that in some cases, at least, he continued (just as Paul himself did) to exercise his occupation.

18

Slaves in the Christian Church

The attitude of Paul towards slavery is a difficult subject. Here his opinions were a compromise between two different forces, or a mean between two extremes. On the one hand, there shall be in the perfect church no distinction of slave and free; all are free, all are on an equal footing in the religion of Christ. "There can be no distinction of nationality nor of sex: there can be neither bond nor free; for you are all one in Christ Jesus" (Gal. 3:28; cf. Col. 3:11). On the other hand, the established social system must not be hastily altered. After all, such a matter as this, which is part of an evanescent and transitional state, should not be regarded as if it were an absolute end in itself. A slave can live a life as truly Christian as the freeman can; and it is infinitely more important for him to live his own life well than to seek for emancipation in the present world. Paul's whole teaching on the subject is an expansion of the Savior's principle: "Seek first the kingdom of God and His righteousness, and all these things shall be added unto you" (Matt. 6:33).

The development of the church, the conquest of the world for Christ: that was the present and instant duty. For that every Christian must work: having wrought out his own salvation, he must work out the salvation of others. To seek to revolutionize the existing system of Roman society could not conduce to that end, but might on the contrary seriously imperil it, and indefinitely postpone it.

Moreover, for a slave to make emancipation and freedom his first aim was a false system of action. To seek to get one's rights is not so important as to learn and to perform one's duties. The former is a narrower and a more selfish aim; the latter is as wide as the universe. The world in which the Christian has to live is evil. His life must always be encompassed with evils. It is of little or no importance to diminish those evils by one. Let him seek the kingdom of God, and the evils will be eliminated as that kingdom is realized on earth. He that loses his life shall gain it; he that sacrifices his freedom for the moment shall gain it in the long run.

Hence is explained the tone of Paul's counsel to Timothy. Not a word is said about the wrongs of slavery, or the right of man to be free. The omission is undoubtedly disappointing at first sight, and the advice given is apt to appear rather temporizing, as if Paul were making terms with evil. Yet when one takes a dispassionate view of the whole situation, one recognizes that the spread of Christianity produced gradually a higher atmosphere of thought in which slavery cannot live. The more fully Christianity is realized in any society, the more thoroughly will slavery be destroyed. It is not yet destroyed anywhere in all its forms; but its worst forms have been eradicated in the most Christian lands, and lessened over the whole world. The duty of seeking to establish equality of opportunities and rights is more generally recognized and admitted than it was in former ages. "Tis something: nay, tis much." Above all, it is now fully recognized that the church should be the champion of freedom; and it is expected that teachers in the church should preach freedom and discountenance slavery in every form. The platform on which human society moves and thinks is now on a higher and nobler level.

Moreover, the historical student who surveys the life of the Roman period must recognize that, if Christian teaching had made the establishment of the kingdom of God its secondary and remoter aim, and had begun by emphasizing the right of every person to be free, slavery would now be as universal as it was then, and there would be no Christianity. The religion which postponed the kingdom of God to the freedom of humanity would have lost its vitality and sunk to the level of other religions; and its history would merely have added one more episode to the story of human degeneration.

Not merely was such an aim as the abolition of slavery in the empire impossible of realization at the time; not merely would the striving after it have sacrificed purposes that were even more noble and more immediately pressing: it could not have been brought about without fighting; and the Christian teaching is against the pursuit of any object which is attainable only through war, especially civil war. It may be questioned by the observer of history whether any of the steps in national progress that have been gained at the cost of war have not been bought at too dear a price. Certainly the price has always to be paid in the long run, and it is heavy; and in the process of payment the value of the step in progress is seriously diminished. In many cases the student of history must feel that the progress might have been more rapid, more beneficial, and less costly if it had been sought by peaceful means and not by war.

Paul advises Timothy to teach that the Christian slave of a pagan master should honor, obey, and respect his master (1 Tim. 6:1; cf. Titus 2:9). It would bring discredit on the church and cause ill-feeling against the church in the society of the Roman Empire if Christian slaves were found to be discontented or disobedient. The slave must cheerfully sacrifice his freedom, reconcile himself to his lot, and do the work that is ordered. The Name and the Teaching will thus be saved from discredit and vilification.

The next part of the advice causes even more difficulty to our modern view. Timothy is not directed to preach that a Christian master should discountenance slavery, or should even set free a slave who is a Christian. One may at first be disposed to think that Muhammad's teaching was better, because Muhammad laid down the principle that a slave who embraces Islam gains his freedom from a Muslim master. But Paul only advises that the Christian slave of a Christian master should serve all the more gladly, because he is doing service and giving help to a Christian; and strongly discourages the slave from showing any insolence, or presuming on the fact that master and slave meet together in the same assembly for common worship (1 Tim. 6:2). It is an opinion too widely spread to be altogether without justification, that mission training of converts in modern times has often tended to produce this temper in them; and the impression has been distinctly prejudicial to the cause of missions.

We must, however, bear in mind that practically Muhammad gave to the slavery of non-Muslims a religious sanction by enacting that slaves were only set free if they adopted the religion of Islam. Islam has been a power that strengthened the hold of slavery on society by formally limiting the right of freedom. The Christian teaching always emphasizes the duties, and discourages the seeking after rights. Cheerful service, renunciation, and self-sacrifice form the lesson that it drives home into the minds of people. All else is secondary. That is primary, for it realizes the kingdom of God. The Christian must trust to the future.

There is, of course, no question as to any discrepancy between the teaching of this epistle about slavery and the teaching of Paul elsewhere. The passages quoted from Colossians and Galatians express the consummation of the perfect church. But in Ephesians

6:5–9 the same practical advice as in 1 Timothy is given in even more emphatic terms. Again, in Philemon Paul sends a fugitive slave home to his master with an apology for his misconduct. He does indeed hint very delicately that the slave might gracefully be set free, but he does not suggest that freedom is his right, or that Philemon should set Onesimus free as a matter of duty. Rather he puts as a personal favor to himself his hope that Philemon will receive the runaway kindly. The "rights of man" are not a Pauline idea; he urges only the duties of man.

The explanation of Paul's teaching about slavery then is that he is wholly out of sympathy with the modern principle that it is our duty to God to resist tyranny by any and every means and at all times. According to Paul, our duty to God is to hasten the realization of the kingdom of God. If resistance to tyranny conduces to that end, then the resistance is right. If submission to tyranny is more conducive, then we should submit. It is a question of means to an end; but the common modern mistake is to treat the means as an end in itself. The teaching of the early church did not make that mistake; if it had, the consequences would have been fatal to the progress of the world.

19

The Time of and Reason for 1 Timothy

First Timothy was written at a time when Paul was at a distance from Ephesus; and though hopeful of soon returning there, he was quite well aware that it might be a long time before circumstances permitted him to pay a visit to that city.

It has been already pointed out in chapter 5 that Paul could not have written this sentence while he had in mind the great scheme (expressed in Acts 19:21, 20:25, etc., and in Romans generally, especially 15:24–26) for leaving the eastern congregations to manage their own life, with the help of letters from himself and of his subordinates, and devoting himself to the establishment of the new faith in Rome and the western provinces. It must therefore have been written either before the scheme was formed in his mind, or after it was abandoned as impracticable and unsuitable. The visit which is meant in 3:14 is not a mere passing or farewell call. It is one intended for definite congregational work, which (if he could have counted on it with certainty) would have rendered unnecessary the careful instructions about church organization given in chapter 2. Such a visit could not have been in Paul's thoughts at any time between Acts 20:25 and the end of the book. It is clear that his whole mind was concentrated during that period on the Roman work (Acts 23:11, 27:24).[1] Nor could any further serious and continued work in Ephesus have been contemplated by him after the great scheme had taken form in his mind. The scheme is sketched in Acts 19:21 and must have been in process of formation sooner. Probably, although his residence in Ephesus (Acts 19:1ff.) was brought to an end a little before he had intended, yet he recognized then that the foundation and establishment of the congregation had been practically completed before his departure. And he had no thought of revisiting the congregation for serious and prolonged work, but had already fixed his mind on new spheres of action, leaving the churches that were already sufficiently consolidated to be cared for by his coadjutors and by their own officials. Corinth still needed a good deal of work, and so perhaps did Thessalonica; but otherwise the year between leaving Ephesus and starting for Jerusalem was spent in the work described in Romans 15:19.

This reasoning compels us to infer that, if the Acts is a trustworthy history, there is no possibility of placing the composition of this first epistle to Timothy at any point between the date of Acts 19:21 and the end of the book.

It is, of course, inconceivable the epistle could have been written at any earlier stage than Acts 19:21. A formed and organized church in full working order is presupposed throughout the epistle.[2] Paul was not writing instructions for a missionary in an inchoate congregation, but for the administrator of a complete *ekklesia*.

We must therefore conclude that the epistle either was written at some time later than the last verse of Acts, or that it is not the composition of Paul but a later forgery; and the latter supposition has been already dismissed as contrary to strong internal evidence.

Something also depends on the exact meaning which we take from the words "shortly" and "tarry long."[3] These words can be used with very different connotations; and in our ignorance of the exact circumstances, it is impossible to say more than that Paul had in mind a return to and residence for some time in Ephesus as a sequel to the work on which he was engaged while writing; but that he was fully conscious of causes for delay which might at any moment come into operation.

If his return is delayed, he wishes that Timothy should have before him an outline of the relation which must exist between the various parts of a congregation or household of God. There are various spheres of duty in an *ekklesia* or church of the living God; and different members must be told off to the different kinds of work which have to be performed. In this allotment of work to suitable persons, and the vigorous orderly performance of it by all, lies the best guarantee for the permanence of the congregation, for the purity of its life, the soundness of its belief, and the vigor of its living faith. The individual can rarely maintain his existence apart from the society of which he is a member. The ordinary man is not strong enough to stand by himself. He is a part of a whole, and not self-complete and self-centered. The Christian ideal differed sharply and diametrically from the Stoic ideal, in spite of many outward and superficial resemblances between them.[4] The Stoic is complete in himself, master of his fate, superior to man and God, independent of circumstances, and able to attain perfection in the development of his own nature. The Christian is a member of a society, namely, the church of the living God; and he is largely (though not wholly) dependent on the maintenance of a healthy life and spirit in that society. The development of the individual is greatly conditioned by that of the society in which he is a part, and in its turn reacts on the development of the society.

It is, however, not Paul's purpose at this present time to insist on what he elsewhere strongly maintains, namely, the influence of the individual on his society and congregation, and the freedom and right of the individual to develop in his own line for his own self through his personal relation to Christ, that is, through faith. There are not wanting suggestions throughout the epistle of this point of view; but it was not the view which needed to be impressed on the administrator of the churches of Asia. In any case it is something outside of himself which is primarily important in the life of the Christian: he cannot attain to perfection through the independent development of his own nature. He must fix his eye and his being on an ideal beyond and apart from himself; he must sacrifice and crucify his natural self in order to attain to the true end of his life; he must live for Christ and in Christ. This end he most easily will attain through the performance of his special duty within his own society, and as a member of that society.

Yet the moment after Paul has enunciated this last idea of the practical means, he is struck with the incompleteness of his statement; and he feels that he must lay additional and special stress on the ultimate aim, the ideal towards which every Christian must strive—the divine Personality which each for himself must live for and in which each must merge his own wretched life, "this body of death." The higher truth and final aim is expressed in a remarkable passage, of rare but not unexampled tone and rhythm in Paul's writings, a passage which has been generally regarded with good reason as a quotation from a church hymn, because it has something of lyric devotional sound and intensity.

The mystery of godliness, the deep-lying idea which brings godliness within the power and grasp of man, is the personality of Christ,

> Who was manifested in flesh,
> Was justified in spirit,
> Was seen by angels;
> Was preached among the nations,
> Was believed on in the world,
> Was received up in glory.

In the first place, is this an extract from a church hymn? Scholars of the most diverse schools and modes of thought are agreed in recognizing the probability that this is so. It would suit the run of the thought admirably that Paul, after emphasizing the importance of the Christian society and congregation for the development of the individual, should express the truth which lies above and beyond this in a formula taken from the church service. Nor is there any probability that already within Paul's lifetime belief had expressed itself in such forms. On the contrary, few will doubt that such crystallization of Christian thoughts in rhythmic form for use in the assembly of the congregation had probably taken place years before his death.

Another view is indeed not impossible, namely, that we have here the beginning of what would develop later into a hymn, and that Paul was transported by intensity of feeling at the moment into an almost lyrical expression of the supreme truth. Some scholars may prefer that view. The probability, however, seems distinctly to lie on the side of the first view, to which the overwhelming mass of opinion inclines. But if that is correct, and if (as we believe), there is here a fragment of a church hymn, then we must draw the full inference from that fact. The church had already accepted universally the marvelous truth of the preexistence of Christ before he condescended to appear on earth.

That thought is, of course, often expressed in the writings of Paul and lies at the basis of his thought. His whole philosophy of life and of religion—the two to him are one—is built upon it. But it would be important to have the further evidence that this same thought was expressed in the plainest terms in a church hymn, sung in the congregations as a fundamental article of the Christian faith, already very soon after the middle of the first century, when probably none of the Gospels in the form in which we have them were actually in circulation,[5] and when many of those persons who had seen Jesus were still alive as witnesses of the actual facts.

So long as it is considered uncertain to what period and author the Pastoral Epistles belong, scholars of all schools will unite in recognizing these words as part of a church hymn. And those who do not like the inferences that must be drawn if the epistles are the work of Paul can at present take refuge in the theory that they were written in the second century, and that the hymn belongs to that period. But the evidence will accumulate, and opinion will finally assume a settled form, that the epistles belong to the period between A.D. 64 and 70. And then the force and implication of the old hymn will be irresistible as to the settled belief in the church from the beginning. What was sung by all Christians in A.D. 65 must have been a fixed belief of all Christians from A.D. 29 onwards. It is impossible to suppose that any momentous change of opinions as to the facts which constituted the basis of the religion can have occurred during that period, while the original disciples were for the most part living.

In the second place, the meaning of the lines quoted requires a short explanation, not as to the religious aspect (which lies beyond the scope of these chapters and which, moreover, is as wide as the Christian religion), but simply as to the mere translation. They are poetic, and we must attempt to think them in prose. They are mystic and transcendental, and we must in a halting imperfect fashion express in more commonplace terms the purpose and order of the thought which they embody.

In Westcott and Hort's edition they are printed as two stanzas; and this arrangement (which seems to be necessary for the right understanding of them) has been imitated above in the present section. The first line, "Who was manifested in material form," implies the previous existence of a being who took on him the form and the nature of a human being in order to become knowable by people. The next line, "He was made just in spirit," must be interpreted in the sense that, though he became a human being, yet he attained the state of being just (i.e., the state of perfection) in spirit (i.e., in his own character and inner nature), not through the striving after an ideal beyond himself (as people have to do), but in the orderly and natural evolution of his own personality.

The stanza ends with the line, "He was seen by angels"; and this line (if the arrangement which we adopt from Westcott and Hort be correct) must be a completion and climax to the first two lines, for the following stanza begins a new series of ideas. Where Paul speaks of the angels, his meaning is peculiarly hard for our modern minds to grasp. He is moving amid ideas which are strange and hardly comprehensible to us, ideas divided from us both by the chasm that separates the Eastern from the Western thought, and by the vast difference between the thought of the first and the twentieth century. For example, who has rightly caught the meaning of "angels" in 1 Corinthians 11:10? I cannot believe that this line of the hymn refers to some single incident or part in the life of the Savior, not even to his ascension into heaven and welcome by angels. It must, as I think, express a third side of his life in material form on the earth, though why such stress should be laid on his being seen by angels during that life, I confess my inability to understand. Perhaps the meaning is that, whereas angels only visit men on special occasions, his life was spent under the eye of angels continuously.[6]

The second stanza describes the effect which his earthly life produced on the world, "He was heralded among nations." The distinction of Jew and Gentile disappears; the hymn is unconscious of any difference: "nations heard the message." "He was believed on in the world," that is, among humanity as a whole: the second line states the result of the first. "He was taken up in glory." When his work was done, he resumed his divine majesty and his divine nature.

20

Warning to Timothy
Against Ascetic Teaching

With the end of 1 Timothy 3 we reach the conclusion of a topic which has been treated in a full orderly fashion, and summed up in a completing and concluding paragraph. One need not, however, expect that the letter should end here. It is not the nature of a letter to expound one topic and stop when the topic has been completed: such a position would be a treatise, not a letter. The writer of the letter now goes on to address his correspondent further.

The prophetic spirit says in express terms that in later times some shall apostatize from the faith. The expression, "later times," has no reference to the end of the world; it only sums up the scope of the prophetic utterance which Paul is quoting.

That some definite prophecy is here alluded to seems inevitable. In a sentence which condemns so strongly all hypocrisy and acting, or playing a part, one cannot suppose that Paul is himself playing a part and quoting a fictitious prophecy. Some utterance to this effect had been made in the Ephesian church, and was well known to the apostle and to Timothy. The prophecy need not be and ought not be interpreted as the forecast of a future that was still distant. It was probably a forecast when it was uttered, but it is now being verified in the experience of the Ephesian church. The present tense "says" ($\lambda\acute{\epsilon}\gamma\epsilon\iota$) is used, not the past tense. The word of God, whether in scripture or in prophecy, is thought of as outside of and unconditioned by time: "God says," "I am," and so on.

If this passage were the only one in the epistle that referred to false teaching, there would be a strong temptation to regard it as referring to a definite tendency and school of thought in the Ephesian or some other Asian church. But the character of the other references to the false teachers forbids this view, which on closer scrutiny does not suit very well the language even in this passage. The "seducing spirits and doctrines of devils" must be understood to describe some species of philosophy or life outside the church, which exercised a misleading attraction on those who were within its bounds. The teachers, who were still within the bounds of the church, caught up this seductive philosophy and practice, and thereby exercised a ruinous influence on some Christians. The pupils went beyond their teachers, pressing the teaching to its logical conclusions and "falling away from the faith," that is, separating themselves from the church and attaching themselves to the sect in which the doctrine and practice took its most logically complete form. That the pupil should carry the lessons of a teacher (whether they be good or bad in their tendency) to a more thoroughgoing extreme than the master contemplated is a common fact, and many examples might be quoted. For example, the pupil of an Anglo-Catholic has often carried the Catholic teaching to what seemed to him a logical conclusion, and joined the Roman Church.

Such a result was actually taking place at Ephesus. The prophecy of the Spirit was the statement of a tendency prevalent at the moment. Paul was wholly occupied in the battle of his own time, and had no interest in warning Timothy against a danger which might become serious in some future period. He is arming Timothy for a war that has already begun, and which will grow more serious if the enemy is not resisted instantly, skillfully, and powerfully.

The teachers who found this teaching profitable and useful for their purpose of obtaining pupils were fully conscious that it was false. They were mere actors, repeating formulas that they did not believe, and thus earning money by means that were disgraceful. They were "branded in their own conscience" as criminals, and knew the brand. Their status as teachers, seeking to attract pupils, has been described in chapters 8 and 9,[1] and the passage 4:1–3 explains more clearly the situation.

The special kind of false doctrine which Paul had in mind is next described. It was of ascetic character, forbidding marriage and prescribing abstention from meats,[2] that is, from certain kinds of food (as, for example, the Pythagorean teaching forbade the eating of beans). He condemns in express terms the second prohibition, stating the noble principle that "everything created by God is honorable, and nothing is to be rejected if taken with thanksgiving" (4:4).

This principle does not imply that there was no reason in the Jewish distinction of foods and prohibition of some foods; but it does imply that no created animal is in itself impure. It does not imply that every kind of animal food should be eaten without discrimination; but it does imply that the discrimination should be on grounds of reason and good sense, and not merely of religious law.

It deserves note that Paul says nothing formally in the way of argument against this misguided prohibition of marriage. Either he regarded that prohibition as sufficiently condemned by its own irrationality and impossibility, and by the previous teaching in this epistle about the duties and qualifications of church officials, or he had some other reason for passing tacitly over the subject, after once declaring in one sweeping statement, that the prohibition of marriage for any class or sect of human beings is a false and demonic doctrine. It is possible in a somewhat lame fashion to extract from the argument about meats an argument about marriage (as many commentators do); but this seems to be a mere makeshift, devised to explain away the contrast between the clear and explicit argument in the one case, and the silence in the other.

Might we not suppose that Paul felt it better to refrain from entering here on this large topic, in which careful distinctions had to be drawn? He had himself in writing to the Corinthians strongly defended the right of voluntary celibacy in cases where one felt that one could serve God better by remaining unmarried. He had even maintained, or at least his words might be understood to maintain, that the life of voluntary singleness was the life of devotion to God, and more honorable than the married life, and that marriage was a concession to the weakness of human nature (1 Cor 7:1ff). There is, I think, no real inconsistency between the teaching of Paul in the two cases. In writing to the Corinthians he had to defend the right of individual choice and initiative against (as I believe) their suggestion that universal marriage would be a salutary rule to prescribe in the church. Here he has to defend human society and human nature against an asceticism so exaggerated as to be unnatural and irrational. But at least some rather full explanation and distinction would have been necessary, if any argument were introduced; and Paul saw no need for an elaborate statement on the subject at this moment.

21

The Words of the Faith and of the Sound Doctrine

An expression like this brings us face to face with the difficulty which weighs, probably more seriously, than anything else with most of those who doubt or deny the Pauline authorship of 1 Timothy and the other Pastoral Epistles. The writer of these letters uses the word "faith" in a different way from the writer of the earlier Pauline epistles. That is admitted. Does it follow that different persons wrote the two series of letters? Is it necessary that, in the case of an idea so wide and comprehensive as faith, a writer must always, in all circumstances and to all correspondents, throughout his life restrict himself to the same side and aspect of its connotation? No one can, I imagine, maintain that Paul must necessarily restrict himself to one use of the term, unless he is also prepared to maintain that Paul was unable to conceive any other aspect of the idea. It is quite common for a man of educated and thoughtful character to use sometimes in one aspect, sometimes in another, a word which expresses a wide and many-sided idea. And it would be mere trifling to maintain that Paul, though quite conscious of the wide range of the word *faith*, always restricted himself to one aspect and use of the term.

We have, therefore, to ask whether there is any probability that Paul was unconscious of the wide possibilities of the term *faith*. Can we suppose that he talked to other leaders, such as Philip at Caesarea and James at Jerusalem, and remained ignorant or unconscious of the different aspect which the idea assumed to them? Even to his devoted follower Luke, as Professor Harnack points out, faith wears a different aspect from what it wears to Paul.

Can we believe that he was able to think out his philosophy of religion, and not realize for himself that faith was a many-sided idea? It seems to me sufficient to put these questions plainly in order to recognize what answer is necessary. Paul was fully conscious that faith wore various aspects to different persons; and it is quite possible and probable that he should have used the word in different ways at different times.

In writing to converts from paganism it is highly improbable that any man would use this term with exactly the same force as he would in writing to Jews. The latter stood on a totally different moral and religious plane of thought; and the higher ideas of philosophic religion could never appear to them in the same way as to those who had been brought up in the colder and denser atmosphere of paganism. In his epistles to the Galatians, Corinthians, and Romans Paul had to rouse first of all in his readers a sense of personal religion, and of the direct relation of the individual to God, which is lacking in paganism and contradictory to its very essence. And he had to rouse and strengthen in the pagan converts an appreciation of the nature and meaning of sin and a desire for righteousness, of which previously even the germ did not exist in their minds. The Jew had already derived from his education in the Old Testament a keen desire for righteousness, a sense of the meaning of sin, and a certain strong abhorrence (more or less strong in different individuals) for sin, though he might often be proud and self-righteous. He was indeed often utterly blind to the sin in himself, but he was keenly alive at any rate to the sin of others.

The conscience and the consciousness of the pagan and the Jew were therefore absolutely different in these respects. Yet both required to have a deeper and stronger desire for salvation and consciousness of the need of salvation; and in both the motive power had to be sought in faith. The faith which must be stirred to life in the Jew wore a different aspect from the faith which must be put into the mind of the pagan.

That the term *faith* is used in the epistle to the Hebrews with a different significance from that which it bears in the Pauline letters is therefore quite natural, and would not constitute by itself (so far as I can judge) any argument against Pauline authorship, if the epistle were written in the style of Paul. It is, however, written in the style of another man.

The Pastoral Epistles are written in the style of Paul; but the word *faith* often wears a different aspect from his earlier letters, though in some cases it approximates closely to the same old sense. This may be a perfectly natural transition. Paul was now writing to the superintendent of a group of churches which were comparatively mature, but which consisted mainly of converted pagans;

and the faith to which he appeals is sometimes the same force as of old, sometimes the externalized result of the working of that force in their society and assembly.

It is not the case that this more externalized conception of faith is absolutely new in the Pastoral Epistles. The transition, or rather the development, towards it can be observed in such passages as Ephesians 4:4—"There is one body and one spirit, . . . one Lord, one faith, one baptism, one God"; Ephesians 4:13—"Till we all attain unto the unity of the faith"; Philemon 6—"The fellowship of your faith." These expressions would be quite natural in the Pastoral Epistles, and would there be taken by most readers without hesitation as implying a more objective meaning of the word than it bears in Galatians, etc.; but they are also quite closely akin to the earlier thought of Paul. In a word, they form the transition and show how the usage of the Pastoral Epistles grew out of Paul's earlier usage. And in those epistles, even without taking into account the intermediate group of letters, the varying sense of the word, sometimes more objective and externalized, sometimes more closely approximating to the earlier usage, is so apparent, that Riggenbach denies the existence of the former meaning, and maintains that faith in the Pastoral Epistles always retains its old Pauline subjective sense. To do this he has to strain the interpretation of some passages in them just as much as several scholars force the natural significance of other passages when they contend that faith in the Pastoral Epistles always bears the objective meaning.

All these attempts to force a single uniform sense on the word do violence to the thought and manner of Paul. It is not a rational method to assume that he must always have used a wide idea like faith in exactly the same shade of meaning. Faith has many sides and many aspects, and Paul was as fully conscious of its manifold nature as any modern commentator.

Moreover, it has been argued that faith in the Pastoral Epistles has lost the unique and prominent position which it occupies in the early letters, and appears merely as one of the excellences of human character. This also is an exaggerated way of putting the case. Faith is emphasized in the earlier letters in a special degree, because it was so necessary in forming the basis of a religious sense among the recent pagan converts (as has been pointed out in the beginning of this chapter). But even in 1 Corinthians occurs the sentence: "But now abides faith, hope, love, these three; and the greatest of these is love" (13:13). At no time in his career did Paul think that faith alone can be made the sufficing solitary basis of the Christian life. When he is urging the supreme necessity of faith, he may be misunderstood as maintaining that faith stands unique and alone, but when he comes to speak of love, he places it even above faith as a needed power in the heart and life of man.

Similarly, in writing to the Greek churches of the Aegean world, after they had attained a certain stage of development, Paul found it needful to insist that the Christian life must bear witness to itself in works and in godliness. He had never thought or implied that faith was sufficient which bore no fruit in life and in act. He had always understood faith to be an intense overmastering fervor which necessarily worked itself out in character and conduct. But he could not do everything at one time for his new pagan converts. He must advance step by step. He must first get the motive power of faith implanted in the pagan mind, and then in the next stage he proceeded to require the further proof and fruit of good works.

So far as the evidence of the Acts goes, Paul did not insist in the same way on the supreme necessity of faith when he was addressing a Jewish audience even in a synagogue of a Greek city. He spoke to the Jews more about the remission of sins: they were conscious of the nature of sin, and they desired righteousness. Both Jews and Greeks needed faith; both needed the remission of sins. But it would be as idle and useless to talk to pagans about the remission of sins before they had begun to realize properly what sin is and what was the relation of each individual to God as it was to talk to the Athenians about resurrection, which they took for the name of a new goddess. Faith alone could supply the force which might raise the pagan mind to a higher level of thought.

The conception of faith expressed in those early letters to the pagan churches implies an appeal to the individual alone. Each member of the church is conceived as coming into direct relation for himself with God; and this idea is so strongly present in Paul's mind that the other relations of life hardly come into his conscious thought. Even marriage comes before him in 1 Corinthians 7 only as it affects the individual. The advice there given implies that each person, man or woman, is to regard the question whether he or she should marry from the individual point of view: does he or she gain more from being married or from remaining unmarried? That this advice may justly be called too hard and too narrow is beyond doubt; that it does not represent Paul's whole mind seems also beyond doubt. The question of marriage is a wider one. It concerns the family and the church. It is not restricted to a calculation of individual advantage, nor did Paul ever think so; but he thought that it was necessary to lay strong emphasis on one aspect of the question on this occasion. He did not attempt to treat, or to lay down any principles about the family, when he was writing to the Corinthians. He was championing the freedom of the individual man or woman. Yet he was not blind to the importance of the family in the organized church; and it is in the Pastoral Epistles that this side of his religious thought comes into prominence. Without those epistles we might take a maimed view of Paul's character and philosophy. They show in what way he regarded the family; and we now turn to this subject.

22

The Family As the Basis
of the Organized Church

One of the most noteworthy features of the first epistle to Timothy, and in a less marked degree of all the Pastoral Epistles, is the emphasis which it lays on the family, as compared with the almost complete silence of the apostle on this subject in his other epistles. So far as I am aware, no one has mentioned this difference as a reason for denying the Pauline origin of the Pastoral Letters. And yet it is probably in this respect that difference of personality might most plausibly be found.

In the first place, we must observe the signs of this difference, and in the second place we can inquire whether the same person at different stages of his career could have varied so much in his outlook on life, on human nature, and on society.

It has been already pointed out in chapter 13 that in the Pastoral Epistles, and nowhere else in his letters, Paul shows an appreciation of the maternal feeling and of the tie that binds together mother and child, and finds in the maternal instinct the divine force and motive power through which the salvation of the woman is wrought out, "if she continues in faith and love and thanksgiving with sobermindedness" (1 Tim. 2:15).

All that was said in that chapter may be assumed here as lying at the basis of our inquiry. The writer who ignores the fact of motherhood has not a broad or a deep conception of the importance of family life; whereas the writer who lays emphasis on the maternal instinct as the central fact and the strongest force in woman's nature is in the way of learning that society must be founded on the family, and not on separate single individuals, if it is to be a well-compacted structure.

It is evident in the description of a bishop's or a deacon's qualifications that his position as the head and guide of a family constituted a most important element in his personal authority. Not merely should Timothy in selecting bishops look for "the husband of one wife"[1] (3:2); the bishop (or the deacon) must be "one that rules well his own house, having his children in subjection with all gravity" (3:4). No one can properly "take care of the church of God" (3:5) unless he knows how to guide his own family rightly. Here is almost an explicit recognition of the fact that the church rests on the family, and is the family "writ large." The church is the family of God,[2] and its members as his children. The latter expression, that the individual Christian is the child of God, may be used without implying in the writer much regard for the importance of the family, for he may be one of those who hold that children ought to be the charge of the community. But no one can logically think of the church as the family of God unless he has a very strong sense of the importance of the family as the unit in the composition of the church.

"Forbidding to marry" (4:3) is mentioned as a doctrine of the most detectable character and a "falling away from the faith" (4:1). A true conception of marriage implies the realization of the importance of the family as the foundation on which the church rests.

On the other hand, a totally different theory is assumed when Paul wrote to the Corinthians: "Are you unconnected with a wife? Seek not a wife; but and if you marry, you have not sinned" (1 Cor. 7:27–28). And when he goes on to describe the mutual relation of a married pair as tending to distract their attention from pleasing God, and to make them "careful for the things of the world, how they may please" one another (7:33). He had then in his mind no thought of marriage and family life as the basis and the essential factor in the constitution of the church. He who rather depreciates the married state as only the second best, and as a concession to the weakness and imperfection of human nature, has an essentially different conception of the nature of the family from that which animates the first epistle to Timothy. In this epistle the family duty is the most binding and sacred. To learn and to practice that duty is the first lesson that children must learn (5:4). He who neglects that duty "has denied the faith and is worse than an unbeliever" (5:8).

So convinced is the writer of this epistle of the rightness of marriage, that he expresses the desire that the younger widows should marry and devote themselves to the family life. Only after they are sixty should they be admitted to consecrate themselves to prayer and works of charity, to living the divine life apart from the work of "ruling their own household" (1 Tim. 5:14),[3] and the special duties of their divine life are "that they may train the young women to love their husbands, to love their children" (Titus 2:5). In other and weaker but more modern words, the woman's separate career, the occasion when she is free "to live her own life" (according to the favorite phrase of the present day), begins in the later years of her life in the world. The earlier part of her life is to be passed in the duties of the family: "she shall be saved through the fact and the spirit and the force of motherhood."[4]

Is this pastoral ideal of Christian life irredeemably opposed to the theory and idea that is expressed in 1 Corinthians? That they are opposed to and inconsistent with one another, so that the same person could not at the same time express them in two letters, must be admitted. But they are not inconsistent in the sense that a philosophic thinker on religion and society could not develop from the "Corinthian" to the "Timothean" point of view; and I think both that the development can be observed in Paul's own writings, and that the traces of the earlier spirit and temper can be detected in the Pastoral Epistles.

In the first place, however, we must always remember that in 1 Corinthians Paul was emphasizing individual liberty against the despotic and arbitrary suggestions of the Corinthian church.[5] He regarded their suggestions too as a slight on himself, both on his authority and on his life; and there is a touch of personal feeling running through the great part of the letter which leads him to emphasize strongly what he has to say in correction of their ideas. Now when a person is speaking very emphatically, he almost inevitably omits to take sufficient account of the opposite point of view, and his expression is apt to become a little hard in tone. That Paul himself was aware of this as he proceeded in his letter is evident from the noble and exquisite panegyric on love, which he introduces in the latter part of the epistle, and which seems unquestionably intended to soften and correct the slight hardness which is perceptible in some of the earlier chapters.

A somewhat similar consideration must be applied in the case of 1 Timothy. If in writing to the Corinthians Paul had to champion the right of personal freedom against a tendency to despotic regulation of the individual life after the fashion of the Roman emperors who thought and provided for their people, in the Pastoral Epistles he has to plead on behalf of law and general principles of order against the Greek tendency to assume too much liberty for individual caprice. Those epistles lay down the general principles on which alone good administration of the Greek churches could be conducted. They legislate for the average man and woman. But would it be safe to assume that the writer had forgotten about the exceptional man and woman? That he had no thought for the divine inspiration which moves the individual occasionally, and which in his earlier letters Paul regards as a supreme law for the person on whom it falls? The Pastoral Epistles omit practically this whole side of church life; but it does not follow that the writer was careless or incredulous of its reality and power. When the inspiration comes, it manifests itself in power; and when it is true, it is not lawless. Although it constitutes and sanctions exceptional cases, it does not override the law; it is in addition to the law and supreme in itself.

In the second place, Paul in writing to the Ephesians regards marriage in a wider view. He compares the relation of husband and wife to the union of soul and body, of Christ and the church. Such comparisons leave no room for the idea that marriage is merely the poorer way of life, to which a man or a woman falls back who is not strong enough for the higher life. They imply that the union of marriage is the divine life and the true harmony of human nature. Soul is not without body; Christ is in the world through the church; husband and wife are one existence on earth. In this view the married pair and not the individual must be the unit in the constitution of the church; and thus emerges the conception which guides the thought of the Pastoral Epistles, that the church is made up of families and that the family forms the basis on which the church is organized.

Yet in this orderly development of idea from Corinthians through Ephesians to Timothy the unity of individual opinion is clearly evident. We have not here an idea developed by a succession of writers: we have the growth of an idea in one writer's mind. The features of the same individual remain in the several stages. The writer of 1 Corinthians had a certain consciousness of the wider idea, which he afterwards declared to the Ephesians, as appears from 11:11, "Howbeit, neither is the man without the woman, nor the woman without the man, in the Lord." We must read these words in the light of the later epistles; and in the same connection we must take Galatians 3:28.[6]

Again, in the later and in the earlier epistles alike we recognize the same strong personality, filled with the prejudice of his early education in Tarsus (where the strictest seclusion and veiling of women, in an Oriental and not a Greek fashion, was practiced) and expressing it in words so strong so to be almost repellent to the modern and Western mind, that the woman was created for the man, that the head of the woman is the man, that the wife shall fear her husband, that she learn in quietness with all subjection.[7] And even in the instructions regarding widows in 1 Timothy there appears in 5:11 a trace of the early opinion that marriage is a mere concession to weakness and less honorable than the life of individual service to the church.

There is, therefore, a fundamental uniformity, amid divergences, in the Pauline view of marriage as it is expressed in all the epistles; and there is no serious difficulty in reconciling the language of all, and no reason to infer difference of authorship from the divergences. The two who marry agree to live one life and not to lead their separate lives, to work with and for each other, to make the family unity and harmony the object—not merely an important object, but the decisive and guiding principle—of their lives. They agree not to pursue separate and inconsistent aims, but to merge their work in the union of the family. This unity and harmony Paul in all stages of his thought proposes to attain through the absolute subjection of the woman to the man, and not through the mutual harmonizing and common development towards a higher ideal on the part of both alike, though there are occasionally found in him some slight traces of the latter idea, which is more in accordance with our modern view. The unity which is attained by subjection of one partner to the other is not so noble an ideal as that which is sought through the growing harmoniousness of two equal partners. But it is easier to attain, and it was in accordance with the facts of ancient society, pagan and Jewish alike.

In the Pastoral Epistles Paul hardly alludes to the voluntary consecration of one's whole life by the individual, separate and single, to the work of the church—except in the case of widows over sixty years of age. Yet in writing to the Corinthians he had laid strong emphasis on this single life as the best and noblest of all. Are we to infer that he had abandoned entirely his earlier opinion, and that he had now in his later years been brought by the experience of life to hold the view (which, as I believe, the Corinthians had expressed in their letter to him) that it was right and expedient to prescribe marriage as the universal rule of the Christian life? That would be a change of attitude too, complete to be reasonably explained as the natural development of thought in the case of a man like Paul. And if it were necessary to put this interpretation on the Pastoral Epistles, I should find it impossible to regard Paul as their author.

There is, however, no reason to regard the Pastoral Epistles as containing a complete statement of Paul's views on the Christian life, or to conclude that any principle which is not laid down in them was rejected by him. They set forth the main and guiding principles of a church organization in respect of the average and general mass of cases. They do not legislate for the exceptional cases. Even in writing to the Corinthians Paul admits that the choice of solitary self-consecration to the divine work must, in the nature of humanity, be a rare and exceptional thing. Such cases form and declare a rule for themselves. Paul's opinion, and the practice of the church (as in the case of the four unmarried daughters of Philip, the prophetesses), were well known; and therefore it was unnecessary (and perhaps, in the Hellenic congregations, inexpedient) to weaken the declaration of the general rule by devoting attention to the exceptions. The Greek spirit was of itself too prone to look to the exception and neglect the rule.

It is an interesting illustration of this subject to note how many of the words peculiar to the Pastoral Epistles (either as used nowhere else in the New Testament or as not used by Paul except in these epistles) belong to the relationship and duties of the family. Paul had no reason and little opportunity for using them in his other letters, since they are taken from a circle of ideas which the other letters hardly touch upon. If we include also terms that belong to the kindred sphere of household economy and sanitation, we have such words as grandchild (ἔκγονον), grandmother (μάμμη), to rule the household (οἰκοδεσποτεῖν), to have dominion over a man (αὐθεντεῖν ἀνδρός), maternity (τεκνογονία), bear children (τεκνογονέω), suitable for old wives (γραώδης is not here used in direct relation to family), youth (νεότης is not used here in direct relation to family), parents (πρόγονοι [includes grandparents; 5:4]), bring up children (τεκνοτροφέω), use hospitality to strangers (ξενοδοχέω refers to the household economy), give charity (ἐπαρκέω [refers to the household economy; 5:10]), wax wanton against (καταστρηνιάω is the antithesis of the true family instinct), idle (ἀγρός), tattlers (φλύαρος), busybodies (περίεργος; these are three vices of the household life), to be a drinker of water (ὑδροποτεῖν), stomach (στόμαχος), master (δεσπότης of household), to do good (ἀγαθοεργεῖν) and ready to distribute (εὐμετάδοτος) and willing to share (κοινωνικός; three words describing a generous and charitable household life), lay up in store (θησαυρίζω), gangrene (γάγγραινα is not here used in direct relation to the household), silly women (γυναικάρια), lovers of pleasure (φιλήδονοι), conduct (ἀγωγή is not here used in relation to the family life), parchments (μεμβράναι), cloak (φελόνη), self-willed (αὐθάδη), soon angry (ὄργιλος), brawler (πάροινος and other faults of life),[8] and aged women (πρεσβῦτις).

This list is a fair example of the causes which largely explain the difference of vocabulary between the Pastoral and the earlier epistles. Some of these words express ideas which are expressed by different terms in the other epistles; but the majority are the names of things or the statement of acts which do not appear in Paul's older writings. It is absurd to quote such words as grandchild, grandmother, parents or grandparents (one single term), as in any way bolstering up a presumption against the Pauline authorship of the Pastoral Epistles. Where could these words occur in the earlier letters? Every epistle has its own special terms. Paul had a rich vocabulary and often varies his way of naming the same ideas or actions or things.

23

Advice to Timothy on the Conduct and Spirit of His Work

First Timothy contains not merely much advice to Timothy as to what he should do and what sort of teaching he should give, but also counsel as to the manner and spirit in which he should perform his duties in the church of Ephesus. The second kind of advice is quite as important as the first, and it is never far away from Paul's mind as he writes. It lurks in, or is at points quite plain in, almost every paragraph; but in 4:6–16 it is especially clear. To do his work is for Timothy not merely the way of usefulness but also the way of salvation. He must have the knowledge of what is right to teach; education, insight, some philosophic aptitude, are good, and in a certain degree indispensable for one in such a position who had to meet those clever false teachers. But these more purely intellectual qualities will have little practical effect without that emotional force which imparts power to the employment of the knowledge. It is characteristic of Paul, and shows the same point of view as appears in the earlier letters, that this driving power, this emotional force, is found by him in the desire for salvation. Timothy is to work to save others in order that he may save himself: "To this end we labor and strive because we have our hope set on the living God, who is the Savior of all men, especially of them that believe" (4:10).

In the last two chapters we saw that the mind of Paul, while he was writing the Pastoral Epistles, was strongly possessed with the importance of the family in the church as a working organization, and that he was not at the moment thinking so much about the individuals who made up the congregation, but rather of the families as the units out of which the church was built up. In the earlier epistles, however, he had in mind more the individuals to whom he addressed himself, and his aim was to awaken in each person, taken singly and alone as an individual, the idea of his own personal relation to God and the consciousness of sin, and so to stimulate in each an intense desire for his personal salvation and a hope of attaining it. In our study of the development of Paul's thought it seemed natural, and in a sense necessary, that his earlier view should be completed by a clearer realization, expressed in the epistles to Timothy, of the relation in which individuals stand to one another in the family and in the congregation.[1]

Now we see that even in the Pastoral Epistles, where Paul is stating so strongly the duty of the individual to the family, he never loses hold on his old idea of what was fundamental. The individual Christian stands in direct relation to God, and must work out his own salvation as the prime purpose which God intends him to achieve. He attains this purpose through full recognition of and respect to his position in the family and the congregation. Nothing can atone for neglect of the duty which each individual owes to the family; there is nothing which is more binding on the individual. With regard to the woman that is to Paul self-evident: she shall be saved through her relation to the family, for the strongest force in her nature runs in this channel (see chapter 13). But equally in respect of the man, he who subordinates his family duty to any other "has denied the faith and is worse than an unbeliever" (5:8).

"Continue in these things; for in doing this you shall save both yourself and them that hear you" (4:16). Such is the conclusion of the paragraph: Timothy shall attain salvation through the diligent and wholeheartedly enthusiastic discharge of his duties (4:15) as teacher and worker in the congregation (4:13), as prophet and guide of the people (4:14), provided that his words and actions show him to the faithful as an example of love and faith and purity (4:12) and hope (4:10). Here we have the "three things that abide—faith, hope, love" (1 Cor. 13:13); and with them is ranked purity. The addition is in perfect accord with the character and teaching of the New Testament generally.

This passage must at once recall to the reader the statement about women in 2:15: they shall attain salvation through the force of motherhood, if they continue in faith and love and sanctification with sobriety. The parallelism is evident, and must be intentional. The difference of career which Paul marks out for men and for women is in accordance with his whole view of life. The care of the family is to absorb the energy of women until the age of sixty. Thereafter she is free to give herself to public work for the church. A man like Timothy (not, of course, every one of the brethren) is to give all his time and energy and thought to reading, to exhortation, to teaching; so that all may observe how much progress in them he makes, and see the way in which his powers and gifts develop in the course of his career. Now development proceeds rapidly and easily only when the individual has found his true line of work.

The true life of the individual, therefore, is the service of the family and of the congregation. There is no inconsistency between the more individual tone of the earlier epistles and the more congregational and family tone of the Pastorals. In serving others we save ourselves. Yet, according to Paul, the starting point of the true life is found in the consciousness of sin and the intense desire for salvation. From the beginning of his career to the end, that conviction is shown in his actions and is expressed in his writings.

We now come to the details stated in this paragraph regarding the conduct and spirit which should be shown in Timothy's work. He should never neglect the *charisma*, the gift which has been bestowed on him, namely, the power of hearing the divine voice and catching the divine inspiration. Here is one of the rare references in the Pastoral Epistles to the gift of inspiration and prophecy; and this gift is alluded to as being so important that no one ought for even a moment to imagine that the paucity of references to it implies any weakening of Paul's earlier belief in its power and immense value. The importance of this gift, and the fact that it is granted to individuals by direct action of God, are assumed in the Pastoral Epistles as familiar and fundamental matters which do not need to be emphasized.

It has, however, been inferred from this and the companion passage, 2 Timothy 1:6, that the gift of prophecy appears in the Pastorals only to embrace a qualification for the work of teaching. Now it is of course true that both these passages refer to Timothy and that Timothy was a teacher; but this gives no justification for the inference that the author of the Pastoral Epistles regarded prophecy as confined to teachers and as merely a qualification for the teacher's duty. In 1 Timothy 1:18 "the prophecies that went before on you" are much more likely to have been made in the open congregation and to be of the same general type that are alluded to in 1 Corinthians. Even if that passage did not occur, and if the two about Timothy stood alone, it would be absolutely irrational to draw such a sweeping negative inference from the silence of the epistles. It would be equally absurd if someone were to argue that the writer of the Pastorals set no store by the Eucharist and regarded it as a worthless and useless ceremony because he never alludes to it as part of the church ritual.

In truth, there is no reason to think that the writer of the Pastoral Epistles differed a whit in regard to either prophecy or the Eucharist from the views stated in the earlier letters of Paul.

Discrepancy has been found between 1 Timothy 4:14 and 2 Timothy 1:6, because in the latter the gift of the Spirit is described as being in Timothy "through the laying on of my hands," while in the former it was given him "by prophecy with the laying on of the hands of the presbytery." The variation might more reasonably be used as a proof that in both cases the laying on of hands is regarded by Paul as a mere accompaniment, and not the cause, of the communication of the Spirit to Timothy. The cause was the divine power alone, but the occasion was on a solemn assembly of the congregation when the presbyters and Paul laid their hands on him. That he sometimes thought and spoke only of the presbyters' hands, sometimes only of his own hands, is in full agreement with many similar variations, where sometimes one detail or aspect of a scene, sometimes another, is emphasized. The situation is similar to that described in Acts 13:2–4 when Barnabas and Saul were sent forth from Antioch (1) by prophecy, (2) at the orders and through the action of the Holy Spirit, and (3) with the laying on of hands of the officers representing the whole congregation.[2]

This passage of Acts shows, further, what is the meaning of the expression "by prophecy" in 1 Timothy 4:14. The appointment of Timothy was preceded and marked out by prophecies, as in fact Paul expressly states in 1 Timothy 1:18. Then followed the solemn meeting in which the action and command of the Spirit, declared through prophecy, was brought into effect and recognition through the laying on of hands by Paul and the presbyters.

The question has also been discussed whether this occasion was at Lystra, when Timothy was first chosen as Paul's companion and coadjutor, or at Ephesus, when Timothy was appointed to superintend that church, or whether both times are referred to. There is no improbability in the supposition that in both cases, at Lystra and at Ephesus, the same events and a similar ceremony took place in the congregation. The context of 2 Timothy 1:6, however, seems to show clearly that Paul there was thinking of the scene at Lystra: the reference to the faith of Timothy's mother and grandmother is decisive. In the passages of 1 Timothy 1:18 and 4:14, there is more temptation to understand that the appointment at Ephesus is referred to, yet even in them I am rather disposed to accept the view of Dr. Hort[3] that the reference is to the original choice of Timothy at Lystra.

It may be asked whether this view is consistent with the account in Acts 16:1–4, where no reference is made to any action except report by the brethren and selection by Paul. But consideration shows beyond all question that that passage gives a very much abbreviated narrative of the facts. It is impossible to suppose either that Timothy's appointment and mission was unaccompanied by religious ceremonies, or that Luke could have imagined that there was no ceremony of consecration and ratification by the local church. The truth is that we must here apply the principle of judging which has been used consistently and frequently in *St. Paul the Traveller.* It was Luke's method, after once describing the procedure in a situation, to assume that the same is understood by the reader in similar situations that follow. There was much that could be assumed as familiar to the audience which he addressed, though now it is unfamiliar to us and has to be slowly recovered from comparison and analogy. We understand, therefore, that the choice of Timothy by Paul was the result of a long process, prophecies designating him, inquiry, testimony, and the final ceremony of appointment by the laying on of hands. This is sometimes spoken of by Paul, as it is by Luke, as the act of Paul alone; at other times participation on the part of the congregation or elders is mentioned.

The meaning of the command in 1 Timothy 4:14 is much the same as in 1 Thessalonians 5:19–20, "Quench not the Spirit; despise not prophesyings," except that there the apostle makes more explicit the fault of belittling and thus discouraging the manifestations of divine inspiration in others, while here he refers to the fault of allowing the gift to grow weak in oneself by want of attention to it. It is a power which is strengthened by cultivation and practice, and is lost if not used.

Those who set so much store on verbal variations and differences between the Pastoral and the earlier epistles may find some cause for suspecting difference of authorship in the fact that the word in the earlier epistle is "make light of" (ἐξουθενέω), whereas that used to Timothy is "pay no heed to" (ἀμελέω), although the meaning is practically the same. But no one who has any literary feeling will object to Paul for possessing a rich vocabulary and for being sensitive to delicate shades of meaning. In the earlier case he censures those who make light of and depreciate with censorious criticism the prophecies uttered by others in the congregation; in the later cases he warns Timothy against failing to cultivate with due care the power of prophecy in himself.

Again, Timothy is advised to show a proper sense of the dignity of his office, and is not to permit overfamiliarity or any want of respect towards himself from any member of the Ephesian church.

Yet this self-respect is not to be exaggerated into overestimation of his office. In the opening of the next paragraph, 5:1–3, we find the counsel that Timothy should show due respect to those who are older than himself. The elder men he is to exhort as fathers, elder women as mothers. One who has been familiar with the ordinary Greek usage in modern times can feel no doubt that these verses imply that Timothy should actually address men and women distinctly older than himself by the titles "father" and "mother"; while he was advised to salute those who were approximately of the same age with himself as "brother" and "sister." It is evident how far this usage is from the Roman Catholic custom that the priest is saluted as "father," even by those who are older than himself and regards all members of the laity as his children.

Evidently Timothy is ranked in this epistle as among the younger, not among the elderly, members of the congregation; that appears both in 4:10 and in 5:1–3. What this implies must be considered in a separate section.

24

The Age of Timothy

In the classification of the citizens of a Greek city there were usually two divisions, the "young men" and the "old men." The most common terms for these two classes are νέοι or νεώτεροι and γέροντες or πρεσβύτεροι. These two divisions of the full-grown citizens were united in separate associations or colleges. The associations of young men were closely connected with the gymnasiums, and their amusements were athletic. They had officials elected by themselves, managing the common funds and the common business; they voted statues to deserving persons, such especially as had given service or brought honor to the *neoi*. They passed decrees, and sometimes imitated the constitution of the city by having their own senate and *ecclesia*. The *neoi* evidently did not correspond to what we call young men; they were full-grown men of military age. And as they grew beyond the military age, they passed direct into the category of the elderly men,[1] *presbyteroi* or *gerontes*, who also had their own club, their own amusements suitable for advancing age, with their own funds and officials. The association of *gerontes* or *presbyteroi* were by far the most influential, and apparently the most wealthy. A society which united in its membership all the men of most experience, and most of those who had held the higher magistracies, naturally exercised great influence in a city.

Those whom we should call "young men" were called by the Greeks *epheboi*. They were regarded as being still in the stage of education in classes[2] under teachers for purposes of physical, moral, and intellectual training. The *epheboi* also had their special organization, their senate and their *ecclesia*, in which evidently they practiced themselves with a view to their subsequent life as citizens. They elected their officials, awarded honors, and passed decrees. As they grew they passed about the age of twenty into the class of the *neoi*.

117

Timothy was reckoned by Paul to be among the *neoi*, or *neoteroi*, the men of active age who should address a *presbyteros* by the title "father." Hence the advice, "let no one despise your youth" (1 Tim. 4:12). This expression has given rise to much discussion and unnecessary difficulty, as if it were strange that Paul should about A.D. 65 consider Timothy among the *neoteroi*. We have only to ask the question, Could Paul by any possibility have regarded him as one of the elderly men or *presbyteroi*? The answer must obviously be in the negative; and the inevitable inference is that he was one of the *neoi*.

The arguments against the Pauline authorship of the Pastorals, based on the "youth" of Timothy, are the emptiest and most ignorant in the whole series of reasoning on that side. The view of Paul was inevitable according to ancient standards of judgment; and it appears not simply in one place (which has been pictured by imaginative commentators as an ignorant imitation of 1 Corinthians by the forger of the Pastorals), but consistently in the advice about conduct in 5:1–3. Paul thought and spoke of him as a *neos*, placed in the rather difficult position of exercising authority over *presbyteroi*.

It is probable that Timothy was very young when Paul first chose him in A.D. 50. Until Paul took him he was under the care of his mother and his grandmother, as is evident from the comparison of Acts 16:2 with 2 Timothy 1:5 and 1 Timothy 4:6. Paul wished to have the molding of his character, and therefore selected one who was little more than a boy. He may have been only eighteen at the time, and it is highly improbable that he was more than twenty.

On the other hand, when Paul left him in charge at Ephesus, we may assume confidently that he was above thirty years old. Not even a companion of long standing could very well be selected for such responsibility as head over presbyters and elderly men at an earlier age.

That appointment was probably made in A.D. 65, and if he was about twenty in A.D. 50, he must have been about thirty-five in A.D. 65. That was an early age for one who had to undertake such duties as Timothy had to perform. He had to exercise some superintendence over the teachers (1 Tim 1:3). He had to exhort the elders, both men and women (but he was forbidden to rebuke them, as being too young to take such a tone to them). The younger men and women he addressed and exhorted as brothers and sisters (5:1–3). He was even expected to reprove the sinful publicly. We, who are accustomed to entrust such duties to boys fresh from college, hardly realize how serious a matter it was in that age and country, when the respect paid to age and experience was so much greater than it is among us. We admit peers to the House of Lords at twenty-one, if their fathers have died, and entrust them at that age with the supreme duties of the legislature, without any sense of incongruity on the ground of youth. Such a thing was impossible to ancient feeling, which regarded seniority as a necessary qualification for a place on such a body.

The very word νεότης, used about Timothy's not yet advanced age, has been counted among the words used only here and never elsewhere by Paul in his letters. But the circumstances prove that, if Paul was speaking so much about the classification by age, there was every reason why he should have occasion to use the noun to designate the position of Timothy among the *neoi*, as he uses it in Acts 26:4 to designate his own early position in Jerusalem.

Titus, like Timothy, was warned to maintain the dignity of his office, which was similar in Crete to that which Timothy filled in Asia. But how different in character are the words in which the warning was conveyed!

Throughout Titus 2 it is evident that the person addressed must rank among the *presbyteroi*, for he is conceived as entitled to address both the elderly and the younger men and women in the same tone, and not like Timothy, who as a younger man was expected to use a different style to the elderly from what he used to those of vigorous age. It was only the man of mature age who was justified by ancient manners in addressing both the mature and those of vigorous age in the same tone and fashion. Slaves are classed in this chapter of Titus alongside of the classes of free citizens, and no difference in the tone of address to them is prescribed. Then Paul sums up in the concluding sentence: "These things speak and exhort and reprove with all authority. Let no man despise you" (v. 15). The conclusion is in perfect agreement with the spirit of the whole chapter. Any possible disrespect to Titus would not arise from his being one of the *neoi*, but from some other cause. It is not merely younger men who fail to make themselves sufficiently respected; men of mature age and assured standing often prove unfit to adapt themselves to a position of authority, and unable to catch that tone of dignity and self-respect, combined with respect for others which impresses all and is well received, yet never admits too much familiarity on the part of any (except those who are lost to shame).

Now compare this with the tone in the corresponding passage of 1 Timothy 4; and one must be struck with the difference amid similarity. The summing up comes first. "These things charge[3] and teach.

Let no man despise your youth; but be an example to them that believe in word, in manner of life, in love, in faith, in purity." It is well worthy of careful observation how this slight difference in the position of Timothy and of Titus affects the expression throughout the epistles. The difference apparently was due solely to difference of age, for if there was any advantage on either side, Timothy seems to have possessed more rather than less authority in other ways, owing to his long and intimate association with Paul. Certainly he plays a far more conspicuous part both in the Acts of the Apostles and in the letters of Paul. The words παραγγέλλω and παραγγελία, referring to the delivery of a message or the announcement of some teaching, are regularly used about Timothy's action, while ἐπιταγη, (used also of God), ἐλέγχω, and παρακαλέω express the style of teaching and preaching that Titus is to assume. The word ἐλέγχω is a strong one: it is once used of Timothy, where the occasion shall demand an especially strong exercise of his authority,[4] but it is three times used to describe the fashion of teaching recommended for Titus (1:9, 13; 2:15). The neutral term is used, as might be expected, about both—twice about Timothy, three times about Titus. As the latter's epistle is much shorter, this implies that if any difference exists, the word was felt to be more suitable for Titus. Διδασκαλία and διδάσκω are often used of Timothy, never of Titus; a young man may teach an old man, or vice versa. But although Paul speaks of the true and salutary teaching (διδασκαλία) which Titus is to enjoin, he avoids the verb and except once (Titus 2:7) even the noun about Titus's work, and favors them regarding Timothy. He uses λαλεῖν, to "preach," twice about Titus, but not about Timothy.

This examination might be carried further, but enough has been said to prove that in an almost perfect identity of subject and instruction the writer of 1 Timothy and Titus (which we may safely take to be almost exactly contemporary) varies the language to suit the varying relation of the two men to those over whom they were to be in authority. Such delicate variations, carried out consistently through two epistles and differentiating so clearly yet with such slight touches the two persons addressed, afford the most conclusive proof that these are real letters addressed by one man to two known persons; and that they cannot be mere compositions of scraps or pure forgeries addressed to names taken out of history.

I have taken no account of 2 Timothy in the comparison, as it belongs to a different moment later in Paul's life, when the feeling and the circumstances had changed. The comparison would, therefore, have to reckon with more complicated factors if 2 Timothy were contrasted with Titus.

Some variations in terms, wholly devoid of significance, occur in these sections of the two letters. The younger class is called in 1 Timothy νεώτερους (5:1) and νεώτερας (5:2), in Titus νεώτερους (2:6) and νέας (2:4). The old women are called πρεσβυτέρας (5:2) to Timothy, and πρεσβύτιδας (2:3) to Titus. Such variations show how the same person may change his terminology from moment to moment.

25

Character of Timothy's Position and Duties

The passage 1 Timothy 4:6–16 mentions the chief kinds of duty in the congregation which will have to be performed by Timothy. These are (1) reading of the Scriptures (whether in public or in private or both is not stated), (2) exhortation (together with reproval of faults), and (3) teaching. To these may be added, as primarily personal but as indirectly affecting the church, (4) cultivation of the gift of inspiration. Elsewhere it is in many passages mentioned or implied that he (and so also Titus in Crete) had a leading part to play in the selection and appointment of church officials, bishops or presbyters, deacons, deaconesses, and widows.

Reading of the Scriptures of course implies much in the way of explanation and interpretation and comment. Exhortation and reproval are often referred to, for example in 3:15, 4:1–2, 6:17, and clearly Timothy was intended to keep an attentive eye on the conduct, the life, and the development of all members of the congregation, so far as possible. Teaching is closely related both to reading and exhortation. The three kinds of work go naturally together, and each helps the other: exhortation and teaching must be based on the Scriptures. Inspiration, cultivated by attentively listening for and expecting the divine revelation, is the condition through which alone these duties can be rightly performed.

None of these partake in any degree of sacerdotal character. All are incumbent on every Christian in the congregation: the difference being that Timothy was to devote his entire time to work in the congregation, whereas ordinary members had other work which required much of their time and attention. That it was a prime duty for every Christian to work and to make a livelihood is not explicitly stated in the Pastoral Epistles, but it is tacitly implied throughout (e.g., 1 Tim.

5:4, 8). And these epistles are in perfect agreement with Paul's teaching in his other letters, and with his practice as regards the obligation to work. Further, the duties of bishops and deacons were in a sense the duties of every Christian, but were incumbent especially on the officials as being more free to give time and attention to them. Those duties then were equally incumbent on Timothy, so far as lay in his power; that is to say, he was expected to exercise a general supervision of and responsibility for their performance by the officials. In this way the supreme direction of the organization of charity and of church business generally must be supposed to lie ultimately with Timothy at Ephesus and with Titus in Crete.

Is it, therefore, safe to conclude that Timothy had nothing in the way of duties of a more priestly type? It would only be safe to make that inference if we could be sure that the epistle was intended to be a complete treatise on the duties of a person in Timothy's position, and that it mentioned every department and class of duty which he would be called on to perform. But that is diametrically opposite to the nature of this letter and of every one of Paul's letters. He has no thought of composing a complete treatise on Timothy's duties. He aimed at giving certain useful counsels, without any thought of completeness.

It is not justifiable then to infer from this epistle that Timothy would not be expected to perform any duties which we should regard as priestly. But we must remember that to the author of Hebrews every Christian is a priest, and that (as the present writer believes),[1] that epistle was written in strong sympathy and frequent communication with Paul, and was approved by him. Every Christian was a teacher, and much more so was Timothy. Every Christian was a priest; much more was Timothy a priest. When a deacon or bishop was appointed, Timothy laid hands on him. So doubtless did the whole presbytery; but Timothy is specially singled out in 5:22, as if he stood out above the others. So Paul sometimes mentions himself, sometimes the presbyters, as laying hands on Timothy; he was above and apart from all, and what they did in association he did as the head of all.

Similarly we must infer that over the whole ritual and order of the church (which is partly described in chapter 2) Timothy was in charge and acted as the one vested with supreme authority. That seems to be implied in 1 Timothy 3:15. We can hardly doubt that, if Timothy were present at the eucharistic meal, it would fall to him either to take the leading part or to delegate it to another. Yet the Eucharist is never mentioned explicitly in the Pastoral Epistles, though I cannot doubt that 3:16 contains a veiled allusion to it, and

3:15–16 clearly allude to knowledge needed by Timothy in his church work.

In short, we must conclude that the silence of the epistle furnishes no negative evidence regarding the extent or character of Timothy's duties. The subject of the priesthood must be treated on other grounds; and the present writer is not competent to discuss it further than the general statement in the last paragraphs. In any such special treatment, it would have to be kept clearly in mind that the organization of the church was still in an incipient stage, and that no hard distinctions had as yet come into existence, such as were enforced in the struggle for existence during later times.

26

The Order of Widows in the Church

The passage 1 Timothy 5:3–16 refers to the widowed women, who have no longer the regular family circle of duties, and who are therefore in an exceptional position. They were naturally so numerous that their position needed some consideration. In the narrow restrictions of ancient social life, it was not easy for them to maintain their children after the earning member of the family had died, and they stood in need of special consideration and help.

The church from the first had recognized that it was bound, as a community, to look after and provide for widows. In Acts 6:1 it is evident that special provision was made to feed such families, and that difficulties were arising as the congregation grew larger and more varied in character. To meet this difficulty the board of Seven was appointed. In Acts 9:39 it is apparent that the widows had certain charitable duties which they performed, and thus something like a rudimentary order of widows, such as was in full vigor during the second century, had come into existence, not merely in Jerusalem but also in Joppa and doubtless universally, in the very earliest stage of the church development.

In this epistle the order of widows is still in a fluid and uncertain condition, and Paul lays down certain principles according to which Timothy should treat these cases.

In the first place, it is assumed as self-evident that all widows must be provided with subsistence (i.e., for themselves and their children). But Paul insists that, where they have children or grandchildren able to help them, it is the duty of these descendants to provide for their parent or grandparent; and it is a sin of the deepest dye to neglect this duty. Church help is given only where private help fails.

In the second place, an order of widows is implied who had forsworn the world and devoted the rest of their lives to church work and charity. Paul is convinced that it would be a bad thing if such widows returned to the ordinary life of the world. They had been admitted to a position of honor and influence on certain conditions; and they must not fall from the performance of those conditions. To prevent such lapse, he would admit no one to the order of widows who was less than sixty years of age, when she presumably had no longer in Paul's estimation any temptation to resume the ordinary social life.

Younger widows he would not admit to the order, but would advise to enter into a second marriage and to devote themselves to the life of the family.

The qualifications of the order of widows are described in 5:9–10. In the first place each widow must have been "a woman of one man." It is clear that this does not mean that she must not have been married a second time, for Paul advises all young widows to marry again; and it is impossible to suppose that he regarded the early death of a husband as a practical disqualification for the order, however good and noble the life of the woman might be. The meaning is exactly similar to the similar expression used about bishops and deacons, and discussed already in chapter 22.

We have already referred to the signs in 5:11–13 of Paul's old dislike and depreciation of marriage, which he showed in his first letter to the Corinthians, as being merely a second-best way of life and a concession to the weakness of human nature.

Then the other qualifications are summed up in the words "well reported of for good works." Like the male officials, the widows must be free from reproach, having a good standing in the congregation, so that their appointment should command general approval.

The qualifications summed up in the brief term "good works" are enumerated more fully in the following words, "if she has brought up children, if she has used hospitality to strangers, if she has washed the saints' feet, if she has relieved the afflicted, if she has diligently followed every good work." The person selected for the order must already have proved in her life a tendency to perform the duties of the widows; and this enumeration may be taken as a fair statement of the purposes which the order of widows was intended to fulfill.

Finally, Paul reiterates that not merely male descendants and relatives, but also female, were under the duty of providing for any widow of their family, and not leaving her to become a burden on the charity of the church.

With regard to the age of sixty at which widows begin to be eligible for the service of the church and for devotion to the divine life and separation from the family cares, a question arises. Was this a point selected by Paul purely from his own judgment and experience, or was it generally recognized as marking an epoch in life, at which retirement from active life and devotion to religious duties might become suitable and proper?

While it is not possible to attain certainty, the second supposition seems much more probable and more in accordance with Paul's principles of administration. Probably those who are better acquainted with ancient oriental ideas about periods in life will be able to quote examples of a belief that the age of sixty was a turning point, where a new life might suitably begin. It is said that the old Hindu law contained the rule of life for men, twenty years a boy, twenty years a fighter,[1] and twenty years head of a household: thereafter one might wisely abandon the life of the world and of business, and devote oneself to the divine life (which to the Hindu meant contemplation and retirement).[2] About A.D. 341 Bishop Eugenius of Laodicea thus retired from active life and adopted the life of a recluse.[3] He must have been not far from sixty years of age then, as is evident from the facts of his career.[4]

Sixty was recognized among the Greeks also as an age when life changed. One who was devoted to the enjoyment of sensual pleasures, like Mimnermus, wished to die when he reached that age. The more vigorous and manly Solon, a true Western in spirit, rebuked Mimnermus and desired to live till he was eighty, and to maintain his activity to the end.

There was evidently some general belief that sixty was the age for entering on the religious life; and this belief was probably not without influence on Paul when he fixed that term for the order of widows. But of course the age was merely permissive, not a regulation of duty.

27

Relation of 1 and 2 Timothy

That there is a certain difference in tone between 1 and 2 Timothy is evident to every careful reader. The first epistle is not so demonstrative in its warmth and affectionateness as the second: its conclusion is by some writers considered to be abrupt and even cold. This difference has been used as part of the basis for an argument that one or both of the letters must be regarded as wholly or partly the work of another writer than Paul. The favorite method in recent criticism of ancient Greek literature from Homer downwards has been to suppose an authentic kernel worked up into a much longer whole, or authentic fragments combined and connected and padded out, by some later hand. By this method it is believed that all the passages which are too clearly marked as Pauline to be denied by a clear-minded and unprejudiced judge can be accepted as authentic, and the rest, which is less plainly Pauline because it adds new elements to our conception of his character and work, can be got rid of and eliminated as a forgery.

The argument that a difference in tone between two letters addressed to one person is inconsistent with authorship by a single writer implies the assumption that a man's tone in writing to a dear friend can never vary, but will always be equally demonstrative in every letter. That this assumption is groundless and false does not need to be proved or urged: everyone knows that the facts of life contradict it. Where a series of letters are written in rapid succession and with a certain continuity of feeling (as, for example, a series of love letters), the tone is likely to be more uniform. But in a case like this, where two letters are separated by a considerable lapse of time, and where the circumstances amid which the two were composed are markedly different, there is not the slightest reason to assume that the tone must be the same, if one author wrote them.

That the ending of 1 Timothy is abrupt is quite true. There is no lingering over the concluding sentences, as if the writer were loath to stop without remembering and saying everything that may show his loving recollection, which is Paul's common method of ending his letters. The fact that the ending is abrupt—it consists of four words alike in the English version and in the original Greek ("Grace be with you"; Ἡ χάρι μεθ᾽ ὑμῶν [6:21])—is sufficient explanation of the want of lingering affection in the leave-taking. You cannot linger long and express much devoted love within four words. Yet an abrupt ending is sometimes enforced or preferred in a letter to the dearest friend.

The whole argument against authenticity, founded on this difference of tone, is composed of statements and judgments made from the wrong point of view. Most of the negative reasoning in regard to these epistles is of that character, as we observe in one case after another. The reader has only to put himself at the right point of view, and everything appears to him in proper perspective, simple and natural. Hence we shall not now stop to inquire whether 1 Timothy is rightly thought to be deficient in affection, or whether it is not rather the case that the intense anxiety which is expressed in the letter about Timothy's successful performance of his task is caused mainly by the very intensity of Paul's love for him. We assume for the moment that the argument is founded on a correct observation, and that the first letter shows less warmth of love than animates the second. The right question to ask is whether the circumstances in which the two letters were written were such as tended to produce some difference in outward expression of emotion. In trying to answer that question we shall attempt to place ourselves at the right point of view; and, in particular, we shall ask whether the abruptness of the conclusion in the first letter was, or was not, likely to arise from the situation and character of the letter.

In the first place we observe that 2 Timothy was written after an absence of some length, when Paul had lost of hope of going to meet his "child." In 1:3–4 he says: "How unceasing is my remembrance of you . . . day and night longing to see you." Yet he knows that he is unlikely ever to revisit Timothy, and he expresses the hope that Timothy will do his best to come and see him. The tone of the epistle is that of a man whose longing to see a dear friend has been growing with time. On the other hand the appearance is that 1 Timothy was written after a comparatively short separation, and that Paul expected within no long time to rejoin his pupil: "I exhorted you to tarry at Ephesus, when I was going into Macedonia. . . . These things write I unto you, hoping to come unto you shortly" (1:3, 3:14). In these circumstances the ordinary man does not give expression in a letter to such strong affection and longing for his friend's company. Moreover, 2 Timothy was written in expectation of early death: the writer was in prison and almost completely solitary. Some of his friends had gone on missions, others had deserted him through fear or through desire to better their condition in life (like Demas). In such a position, with death before him, the ordinary man is more prone to express his desire and longing for the presence of an old and tried friend.

In the second place, Paul had a distinct reason for writing his first letter to Timothy, and that reason was not purely personal. It is evident to every reader, and has been shown at length in these pages, that the apostle was full of anxiety about Timothy's work in Asia; that he was apprehensive lest his pupil's retiring disposition and want of confidence and boldness might lead to his being pushed aside and not properly respected among the clever and fluent and audacious Hellenes of the great Greco-Asian cities; that he was impelled by the deep affection which he felt for Timothy to write a letter of advice and stimulus. In the first epistle the charge to Timothy as a manager of a great office guides Paul's whole thought, and the personal feeling towards a pupil and friend is submerged, though it influences the writer's mind. In the second epistle the affection for Timothy dominates Paul's mind, though never to the exclusion of the charge with which Timothy is entrusted.

Accordingly, the second epistle is far more personal to Timothy: it shows him far more as a human being in his relation to other human beings, and especially to Paul himself. Take, for example, the paragraphs from 1:3 to 2:13; how full they are of touches personal to Timothy as Paul had known him, and to Paul in his relations with Timothy. So also 3:9–17 and 4:5–22.

In the first epistle, on the other hand, while the personal element appears in a similar way in 4:12–16, 5:22–23, and 6:11–14, yet in all of these the charge entrusted to Timothy is also prominent and sometimes even dominant, whereas in the passages just mentioned from the second epistle, the charge appears rather as the underlying anxiety, and the personal feeling is dominant, sometimes entirely, sometimes less completely. In other parts of the second epistle the charge is more prominent, and the personal element almost disappears from view just as in the first: such are the paragraphs 2:14, 3:9 and 4:1–5. The spirit of the two letters is quite similar, deep affection combined with great anxiety about Timothy's success. But in the first letter the anxiety is so great as to submerge the affection, while in the second the love often dominates and over-powers the anxiety.

There is not in 1 Timothy the same repeated conjunction in one sentence of Paul and Timothy as in 2 Timothy. Where personal affection is dominant, the expression tends to bring together the two persons. Hence this difference, which any reader will be able easily to prove by statistics, is the natural result of the general situation.

This observation clears away a discrepancy as to fact, which has been found between a statement in the first and a statement in the second epistle. In 2 Timothy 1:6 Paul speaks of "the gift of God, which is in you through the laying on of my hands." On the other hand, in 1 Timothy 4:14, this same gift was given Timothy "by prophecy with the laying on of hands of the presbytery." There has been much discussion of the seeming contradiction between these two passages; but when they are contemplated from the right point of view, there is no contradiction and no discrepancy.

The truth is that the form of appointment always included two distinct parts: (1) the action of the Holy Spirit and (2) the action of men, namely (Paul and) the official authorities of the church in conjunction. The typical case is the choice of Barnabas and Saul in Acts 13:2. Applying this general rule of appointment to the special case of Timothy, we may say with perfect confidence, in the first place, that Paul assumed the general form to have been followed in Timothy's case, and secondly, that every reader and every Christian at that period had the same knowledge in his mind. In Timothy's appointment the Holy Spirit, Paul, and the official authorities of the congregation had all cooperated. There was no need for Paul to mention in detail all the parties concerned in the selection and con-secration of his pupil. Where Paul is thinking specially about the close personal relation between himself and Timothy, where he tends repeatedly to conjoin Timothy and himself in one sentence, he speaks simply of "the laying on of my hands," knowing that Timothy will understand the whole situation described (so in 2 Timothy 1:6). He emphasizes the personal relation between him-self and his pupil, and the other parties disappear out of the lan-guage. Where, however, Paul desires more to lay stress on the solemnity and the authoritative character of Timothy's appointment, he mentions the conjunction in that action of the Holy Spirit, "by prophecy," and the presbytery, while he himself sinks out of the sentence (as in 1 Timothy 4:14). There is found to be perfect har-mony between the two allusions as soon as we place ourselves at the right point of view. The omission of details in a complicated yet familiar picture is constantly observable throughout the New Testament.

The differences between the epistles are not only slight in themselves, but fully accounted for by the difference in Paul's position as he wrote. Amid the superficial differences the fundamental identity of feeling in the two epistles is quite clear. The relation of Paul as master, teacher, and spiritual father to Timothy is clearly shown throughout the first epistle, from 1:1, "Timothy, my true child in faith," and 1:18, "my child Timothy," to 6:21, "Grace be with you." While Paul is full of anxiety that Timothy shall discharge the difficult duty successfully, the anxiety is tempered by his deliberate judgment and confidence that the younger man will acquit himself well. Chapter 6:20–21 is full of that confidence: some have erred, but Timothy will not err or misunderstand his charge. Timothy is addressed as "man of God" (6:12). While Paul expected that the Asian Christians should look up to Timothy, and that Timothy should exact from them the respect due to his position (4:12), he was careful to show by this address that he paid to Timothy the same respect which he expected that the Asians should pay. He knows that Timothy has been called to the eternal life and has borne testimony to the truth in the sight of many witnesses (6:11–12), and he remembers "the gift that is in" him (6:14).

While it is true that the second epistle gives more prominent and emphatic expression both to the affection and to the respect which Paul felt for Timothy, the expression moves along very similar lines: "beloved child" in 1:2 and "my child" in 2:1. Timothy has "followed my teaching, conduct, purpose, faith," etc.; he knows what he has learned and been assured of from childhood. It is suggested, though not expressly said, that he is the "man of God furnished completely unto every good work" in 3:17. He is contrasted with those that "turn away their ears from the truth, and turn aside unto fables," with perfect confidence that he will "fulfill his ministry" (4:4–5). Paul knows and reminds him of "the gift of God which is in you" (1:6).

Again, while it is clear that Paul in the first epistle more emphatically and repeatedly expresses his anxiety in respect of Timothy's shyness, timidity, and too retiring disposition, lest these faults may betray him into shrinking from fully and efficiently discharging the duties and using the powers of his office, yet it is quite clear that in the second epistle the master entertains the same apprehensions about his pupil, and thinks the same warnings and encouragements are needed. Timothy must be on his guard against "a spirit of fearfulness"; he must cultivate "a spirit of power and love and discipline"; he must "stir up the gift of God, which is in" him, and not let it grow weak from disuse, as might happen to a person in whom too great shyness and lack of confidence hindered the expression of the gift.

There is actually a fault in Timothy which is more distinctly hinted at in the second epistle than in the first. The false teachers, clever, fluent, and versatile, whose probable opposition and disrespect to the modest and not very highly educated Timothy caused such apprehension in Paul's mind, figure in the second epistle almost as prominently as in the first. The same kind of fear about Timothy's power to maintain the fight against them troubled Paul in both letters. In the second he gives even clearer expression to one danger which might result to Timothy from this opposition, owing to his special character. One who is disposed to be too backward and slow in meeting the opposition may readily fall into the error of losing his temper. He endures it until it has provoked him to anger, and he begins the struggle only after he has been enraged, whereas "the Lord's servant must not strive, but be gentle to all, apt to teach, forbearing, in meekness correcting his opponents; if perhaps God may give them repentance unto the knowledge of the truth and they may recover themselves out of the snare of the devil" (2:24–26). Thus it might come about that Timothy, too shy and timid and (in outward appearance) meek, should fall into the opposite fault of quarreling; and he is cautioned against it.

If one is on the outlook for contrast and difference between the first and the second epistle to Timothy, a far more striking divergence of tone is apparent in another direction, which will form the subject of the next section.

The abruptness of the conclusion in 1 Timothy is in accordance with the rather disjointed character of the letter. As has already been pointed out, Paul wrote it probably in parts, not continuously.

28

The Thought of Death in 2 Timothy

As was natural in Paul's situation, with his own death imminent before him, his mind turned much while he was writing the second epistle on the thought of death and of the last times. He remembers what was and had always been a central idea in his teaching, that Christ Jesus had "abolished death and brought life and incorruption to light" (1:10).

The expression "against that day" or "at that day," referring to the day of judgment, occurs three times in this epistle. Paul does not use it in 1 Timothy nor in any other place except 2 Thessalonians 1:10. The second epistle to the Thessalonians is for different reasons much concerned with eschatological ideas, the day of judgment, etc.

His dead helper and comforter Onesiphorus is referred to in very affectionate terms (1:16–18). The words indeed do not inexorably prove that Onesiphorus was dead, if one is strongly inclined to judge otherwise; but they are of such a character that I feel less doubt on the matter the more often I read the epistle as a whole and take them in their context and surroundings.

He thinks much in this epistle of what comes after death. He endures all things, in order that the elect "may obtain salvation with eternal glory: faithful is the saying" (2:10).[1] Then follows (vv. 11–13) what has by some been taken as a hymn:

> For if we died with him, we shall also live with him;
> If we endure, we shall also reign with him;
> If we shall deny him, he also will deny us;
> If we are faithless, he abideth faithful;
> For he cannot deny himself.

In a very similar passage of 1 Timothy 4:8–10, the object and purpose and effect of godliness is found in the "promise of the life which now is, and of that which is to come" (v. 8). Paul's mind was not so filled with the thought of death when he wrote that epistle: if he had been then in the same frame of mind as when he wrote the second epistle, "the life which now is" would have had no part in his thought, and he would have regarded godliness as desirable for the eternal glory. So again in 1 Timothy 6:19 "the time to come" and "the life which is life indeed" are vaguely presented to the reader because they are not at the moment vividly present in the writer's thought. It has even been suggested by some writers that the "life which is indeed" may quite well mean simply the real Christ-like life on earth, but this view appears incorrect.

In the second letter to Timothy, Paul thinks much of what will happen in the last days (3:1–9 and 4:3–3). There shall be a season when the power of evil is exalted, and when sin seems to be triumphant; but this shall be the beginning of the end. Then, as is invariably the case in the apostolic writings, with the thought of that last time and the end of the world, comes also the thought that not merely is it coming, but it is even now. The evil and folly and crime of the present day is the herald and proof of what is coming; and the false teachers against whom Timothy has to contend serve as examples of the exaltation of the power of evil. The apocalyptic visions and the eschatological teaching of the apostle always tend to express themselves in the present tense; and this has misled many modern scholars into the false idea that the apostles believed the end of the world to be imminent and likely to occur in their own lifetime. Those scholars misunderstand the ancient form of thought, which expresses absolute certainty and eternal truth under the form of present time.

Similarly in 4:1–4 the thought of the judgment day and the appearing and kingdom of Christ on earth forthwith calls up the associated idea of the temporary triumph of evil which will precede and herald it; and this triumph is described after the analogy of the false teachers at the present moment. But in 1 Timothy 6:14 the appearing of Christ is remote, which "he shall show it in its own times" (v. 15); and it is only spoken of as the term of an irreproachable career. The growth and power of evil is mentioned also in 1 Timothy, but simply as a fact of the future and not as connected with the appearing of Christ in judgment (4:1). It is regarded as the natural and foreseen development of the false teaching, which must proceed in its course of wrong.

That the same person should in one mood and frame of mind think and speak of the judgment day as distant, and in another mood as imminent and immediate, is thoroughly characteristic of human nature and of the New Testament style.

The words, both verb and noun, for death occur far more frequently in 2 Timothy than in 1 Timothy: θάνατος, νεκρός, and ἀποθνήσκειν (in a compound) are only found in the second letter.

In the first epistle Christ is thought of mainly as the Savior of people in the world; see 2:4, 3:15–16, 4:10, 5:4 ("unto eternal life," however, in 1:16). He shows what one must do to be saved, and how one must live to be saved.

There is nothing to wonder at in this general contrast between the epistles: it only mirrors the difference between the situation and emotion of Paul on the two occasions. The words of 2 Timothy 4:6–9 show what he thought of his situation then, "I am already being offered, and the time of my departure is come." In the first letter the thought of stimulating and encouraging Timothy to perform successfully his duties in Asia overpowers every other thought. Timothy must work right on to the end. In the second letter the same thought is not lacking. It appears constantly throughout the first four chapters; but the expression of it is colored in a totally different way, and the explanation of this coloring does not become apparent until we come to 4:6–9. Then we see that the idea of 4:6–9 has been latent in Paul's mind throughout the first few chapters. This idea constitutes the unity of the second epistle. It lies hid for a time, traceable only through the tone in which other ideas are expressed. Then it forces itself to the surface, and Paul thereafter gives free course to the consequences which it brings with it. He would rather see Timothy before he dies.

29

The Pauline Philosophy of History As Expressed in the Pastoral Epistles

Throughout Paul's earlier letters there occur frequent expressions which reveal his way of regarding history. To his mind the soul of history was the will of God. Do we find the same view of the world in the Pastoral Epistles? We may start by quoting one or two examples of the style in which he expresses his philosophical theory of the progress of human history. In Galatians 1:15 he says, "When it was the good pleasure of God, who set me apart even before my birth, and called me through his grace, to reveal his Son in me, that I might preach him among the Gentiles"; in Galatians 4:4, "When the fullness of time came, God sent forth his Son, born of a woman, born under the law, that he might redeem them which were under the law"; in Colossians 1:26, "to fulfill the word of God, even the mystery which has been hidden from all ages and generations, but now has it been manifested to his saints, to whom God was pleased to make known what is the riches of the glory of this mystery among the Gentiles, which is Christ in you, the hope of glory"; in Ephesians 1:11, "in whom also we were made a heritage, having been foreordained according to the purpose of him, who works all things after the counsel of his will."

The whole philosophy of history is expressed in such sentences as those. To Paul's mind the process of human affairs was the gradual evolution of the divine will within those conditions of time and space that hedge us in. According to his view, the coming of Christ is presented to us as the culmination of the older period of history and the beginning of the new period. The older time leads up to it and finds its explanation in it; the later stage starts afresh from it. Thus the purpose of God is unfolding itself in all the events that go on around us.

Like the greatest of the Greek philosophers, Paul was profoundly sensitive to the flux and change and transiency of all earthly phenomena: as the old Ephesian said, "All things are in transition," and "You cannot step twice into the same river." Only the divine then is true and real and permanent. The moral side of this idea was especially strong in his mind, "He sighed, as scarcely any other has done, beneath the curse of the transiency of all that is earthly."[1] Under this uncertainty and change Paul saw that there lay the one real and cognizable truth, namely, there is a purpose and a law which works itself out amid the flux of things. The change was subject to a law, and this law was the purpose and will of God, present with him from the beginning.

The form in which this idea is expressed by Paul is profoundly influenced by Greek thought. That the divine power molds the affairs and actions of people as the potter molds the lifeless clay is the Hebrew way of expressing the idea. The Greek philosophers and poets—those of them who were the greatest and most characteristic Greeks—recognized that the will of God acts through the actions of living and thinking persons, as a law which they unwittingly obey and work into actuality, though they think they are acting for their own purposes and ends. Hence Homer already regards the whole tangled and confused web of the conflicts around Troy as the gradual realization of the predetermined will of Zeus. The last words of the opening paragraph of the Iliad are Διὸς ἐτελείετο βουλή, i.e., the will of the Supreme God was worked out to its consummation, or in more modern and abstract philosophical language, the soul of the story was the will of God. The will is preexistent: it becomes evident to man only as it is worked into history.

Now since the divine will is always true to itself, and neither varies nor changes but is a uniform law of growth, it follows that, if once we catch even a glimpse of it at any moment in history, that momentary glance is true for all time. And hence we may learn to read the real character of this present time, and we may forecast dimly the possibilities that lie before us in the future by looking back into the past.

What then in Paul's estimation had been this purpose of God, which had been working always in the world, not understood by people at the moment, but now clearly revealed to those who had been illuminated by the radiant truth of the message that had come?

In the pagan world, amid which Paul was born, the feeling had gradually grown strong and taken possession of the popular mind, that the world was steadily degenerating into ruin and decay, and that no relief from the universal uncertainty, strife, and cruelty could ever be attained by ordinary human means. The old order could not be improved into a better system: the path of revolution only made greater confusion.

Such appeared then the issue to which civilization had led in its chief centers, Greece and Rome. It had resulted only in misery, crime, bloodshed, and deterioration. On that all were agreed. It seemed to turn its back on the divine life, to move further and further away from God, and to prefer the madness and recklessness of man to the divine peace. Except in the appearance of some God on earth, there was no help possible.

All people were praying and offering vows for "salvation." In city after city and village after village of the Greco-Roman world, especially in Asia Minor, the explorer of that world is impressed by the number of dedications and offerings, beseeching for "salvation" (σωτηρία). This was what Jesus brought, and Paul preached. Those pagans prayed for they knew not what. They asked for salvation; but they did not know in what salvation lay, or what was its nature. What they ignorantly sought for, Paul declared unto them.

Paul was never hampered by the difficulty, the greatest with which the modern missionary has to contend, of learning how to understand the pagan mind and how to touch the pagan heart. He had grown up in familiarity with the pagan mind. He knew from childhood its way of looking at life, what it dreamed of and longed for. He knew how to make his ideas intelligible to the pagans around him. A Tarsian, he knew the thoughts of the Greek East. A Roman, he had caught something of the Roman spirit. Amid Greeks and Romans he moved as one at home in a familiar world; and he played on their hearts as a musician on his instrument. He set before them the *soteria*, the salvation, for which they were praying; and they found the salvation which he declared more satisfying, more ideal, more perfect, than they had been able ever to imagine.

While most of the poets, the half-prophets of the pagan world, declared that salvation was impossible because human means had failed, Virgil, the herald of the New Empire, found it in the triumph of the New Age. The New Rome would regenerate the world, because it was the creation of the divine power present on the earth. Gradually this idea, first expressed in the fourth Ecologue, crystallized into the doctrine of the divinity of the emperor; and even in this vulgarized and petrified and lifeless form it was still a power.[2]

Paul felt deeply this spirit of his age—the conviction that things had gone wrong; that the world had failed and was growing worse; that only through divine aid could progress be made and sin shaken off. He called the evil of the world "sin"; the pagan nations called it by other names. There was this profound difference between him and them, that he regarded the fault and the cause of evil as due to man. The pagans regarded it as due to fate or to God or to chance, and recognized no fault in themselves. In the early chapters of Romans, where Paul states his view most fully and clearly, he assumes straight away that the end of man and the aim of human life is to be righteous, and the reason why he has failed lies in himself.

Paul too, like the poets of the New Empire and the New Rome, saw the salvation of humanity revealed in the manifestation of divine nature incarnate in human form. This was the purpose and will of God from the beginning of the world. To bring about this "in the fullness of the time," when the world had become convinced that it was the only way, had been the plan of God throughout the evolution of human history. Towards this all the past had been tending. This was the law which lay underneath the apparently lawless and hopeless welter of bloodshed and misery that constituted the history of preceding time.

The triumph of the divine purpose, the object which the divine will was working out, was the cross of Christ. This cross recalled to the mind of Paul, the Greek and the Roman, that stump with crossbeam on which the *tropaeum* and spoils of battle were hung after the victory had been gained. The decree of fate, the unfulfilled and forfeited bond in which the curse and destruction of man's efforts was expressed, was nailed to the cross, as the Roman conqueror fastened to the crossbeam and the upright beam the spoils of his defeated enemy (Col. 2:14). The victory of the crucifixion was the declaration of the will of God, the explanation of all past history and the new beginning of all coming history. The erection of the trophy culminates finally in the long train of the triumphal procession, in which the subordinate powers and the captive enemy were led up to the capitol and offered to the supreme God (Col. 2:15).

This doctrine of Paul is as clearly and emphatically expressed in the Pastoral Epistles as in any of his writings. The purpose of God was working from the beginning, and therefore his kindness and grace towards people were always active, but had become patent and intelligible to them only through the death of Jesus. "The grace which was given in Christ Jesus before times eternal, but which has now been manifested" (2 Tim. 3:9); "Jesus, who gave himself a ransom for all, the testimony to be borne in its own times, whereunto I was appointed a teacher among the Gentiles" (1 Tim. 2:6); "The hope of eternal life, which God, who cannot lie, promised before times eternal, but in his own seasons manifested" (Titus

1:2–3). This promise of God, given and published long before, had never been rightly understood until its true meaning was declared through the crucifixion.

This Pauline view is fundamental in all the Pastoral Epistles; but it is not stated there as a truth needing to be emphasized by the writer. It is rather brought in incidentally as a familiar principle. It is appealed to as something well known to Timothy and Titus, and accepted by them as an axiom from which inferences may be drawn and by which further principles may be tested and proved. That is "the mystery of godliness" (1 Tim. 3:15), now made plain, was formerly obscure.

But it is argued by many modern scholars that the very word "godliness" is not Pauline. It is strange to his vocabulary in the older epistles; and since it is common in the Pastorals, it stamps these as the work of some other writer. But this word "godliness" (εὐσέβεια) is one of the most characteristic words of pagan religious thought. Could Paul, who knew the heart of paganism so well, and who through that intimate knowledge was marked out as the one man that was qualified beyond all others to explain the gospel to them—how could he be ignorant of that word? And knowing it, how could he fail to speak of it to those who eagerly desired to realize it? In the opinion of the present writer it would be a strange and inexplicable thing if Paul in placing his gospel before the pagans of the Greco-Roman world had never used a word which lay so close to their hearts. They thought that people should and must be "godly" (εὐσεβεῖς) that "godliness" was a quality essential in a good man. Paul explained to them in what "godliness" (εὐσέβεια) consisted, and how it was to be attained—just as he did with "salvation."

Why then is it not found in the earlier epistles? I doubt not that it was used by Paul often in oral address to the Asian and Galatian and European churches; but in the letters it was not in keeping with the special message which at the moment had to be emphasized to them. The full answer to this question would require an exposition of the topics and treatment of every letter. The Pastorals, here as in so many other cases, intervene to complete the picture of Paul, and to show him as in every respect the apostle to the Gentiles, who showed them that faith was the force which produced for them both salvation and godliness.

30

The Office of Timothy in
Ephesus and Asia

In 2 Timothy 4:5 Timothy is said to be a *diakonos*. Here Paul, after sketching an outline of Timothy's duties—"Preach the word; be instant in season, out of season; reprove, rebuke, exhort, with all longsuffering and teaching . . . be sober in all things, suffer hardship, do the work of an evangelist"— adds as a climax the brief summary of these instructions, "fulfill your *diakonia,*" that is, perform the whole duty of your office and charge.

Very similar is the thought in 1 Timothy 4:6, "If you put the brethren in mind of these things, you shall be a good *diakonos* of Christ Jesus." This also is a summary of the instructions given in the preceding paragraphs. Insofar as Timothy performed all his duties, he was a good *diakonos*.

Accordingly, if Paul applied any special term to Timothy's range of duty and authority in Asia, he would call him a *diakonos*. What is the significance of this term? The answer is not easy, but no one hesitates or can hesitate at least about one thing: here *diakonos* has not as yet become a strictly technical term, indicating a specific office in a hierarchy.

Paul calls himself "a *diakonos* of the gospel" in Ephesians 3:7 and Colossians 1:23; in Colossians 1:25 and in 1 Timothy 1:12 he names his sphere of duty *diakonia*. The use of the two cognate words regarding himself is exactly parallel to the use of them regarding Timothy;[1] and it seems beyond doubt that Paul considered his coadjutor Timothy as engaged at Ephesus in the same species and kind of duties as he himself performed in any place where he chanced to reside and to find "an open door." Hence the description of Timothy in 1 Thessalonians 3:2 as "our brother and *diakonos* of God in the gospel" is quite in keeping with Paul's language elsewhere [though

142

the reading there is uncertain, as the variant "fellow worker with God" (συνεργός) has good authority to support it]. Similarly Tychicus is "the faithful *diakonos* in the Lord" (Eph. 6:2; Col. 4:7). There can, therefore, be no doubt that the whole class of duties performed by Paul himself and by those whom he trained to be his coadjutors was summed up by him as *diakonia*.

One can hardly doubt that this use of the word *diakonos* is older than the employment of the same term to denote a definite office in a congregation. Yet, alongside of this more primitive use, we find the term employed in a more sharply defined fashion. There are various passages in Paul's letters where *diakonos* is really a title and technical term for an office in the congregation, for example, 1 Timothy 3:8, 12; Romans 16:1; Philippians 1:1. I cannot feel any hesitation in separating these passages from those quoted above. In the one class the *diakonoi* seem to be resident and settled officers of the congregation, lower in grade than *episkopoi*. In the other class Paul and his coadjutors, who represent him in his absence, are *diakonoi*; and to this class must be added Colossians 1:7 (Epaphras) and 1:25 (Paul) and 4:17 (Archippus).[2]

That the word *diakonos* in ordinary usage implies service, humbler rank and submission to order, is quite certain. This was the term which Paul chose as suitable to mark his place and duties among his congregations, and to describe the charge which he gave to his coadjutors over one or more of those congregations. The thought in his mind was the teaching of Jesus, for example, "The greatest among you shall be your *diakonos*" (Matt. 23:11); "whosoever shall humble himself as this little child, the same is the greatest in the kingdom of heaven" (Matt. 18:4). The same thought lies in the pope's title, *servus servorum Dei*.

No one can fail to observe the marked analogy between the passage above quoted, Colossians 4:17, and the character and spirit of the letters to Timothy. What was needed in the way of message and instruction for the congregation at Colossae was stated in the letter to them and in "the epistle from Laodicea" (v. 16; i.e., Ephesians). But beyond this there was something required in the way of special message to the *diakonos* who had charge of the congregation of Colossae. This Paul conveys in one brief sentence, "Say to Archippus, Take heed to the *diakonia* which you have received in the Lord, that you fulfill it." In this short message is implied all that is contained in the Pastoral Epistles and much more. Paul had in mind the kind of message that is suitable for a person charged with the responsibilities of Archippus; such a message might fill a large volume, or it might be compressed into a single short letter (like that addressed to Titus), or into a longer letter (like 1 Timothy), or it might be expressed in a brief reminder (like that sent to Archippus).

One cannot, therefore, for a moment doubt that if Paul had sent a letter direct to Archippus, it would have been in the style of the Pastorals, something differing in style and kind from Colossians and Ephesians. The very fact that an extra message is sent implies that those two epistles did not contain what was needed for Archippus.

In this case, however, Paul did not send a letter. He trusted that Archippus would catch what was needed from this brief message, and from the commission which the latter had originally received. The brief message was intended to strengthen in Archippus' mind the spirit of former teaching. Archippus needed only to recall the charge which he had received, and to give attention and care to it. The duty and the teaching were in his mind; he had only to keep the instruction fresh and strong there. The teaching then was all-important and complete; there was in a sense nothing to add to it. It is simply the "sound doctrine" and the "faithful saying" of the Pastorals. The minister and teacher must hold fast to this: if he does so, the rest will come to him of itself through the Spirit.

There is, of course, much more involved in the ministry as Paul conceived it. In a sense, there was much to add; but it will add itself, if the "sound doctrine" is clearly understood and firmly grasped.

It stands to reason that the *diakonos* in charge of one or more congregations would require a special and different message from that which was most appropriate for a congregation or for several congregations. Archippus, like Timothy, would doubtless have been reminded, if Paul had written the letter to him, of the general principles that were likely to be serviceable in the practical work of guiding a congregation. Not exceptional cases, but general rules, would be stated. Legislation is for the average and the mass of men. The exceptions have to be considered and treated singly by the good sense of the "minister" (*diakonos*) and especially through the constant help and guidance of the Spirit, which Timothy is directed repeatedly to listen to and wait upon. For these exceptional cases Paul, therefore, lays down no rules. They will carry with them their own justification and their own standard. The family is the basis of Christian society: that is the safe principle in practically directing a congregation. Paul makes no allusion to the idea which is so much emphasized in 1 Corinthians 7, that in some cases the highest level of life for certain individuals lies in perfect celibacy and devotion to the divine life. Those are cases of exceptional individuals, about whom the Corinthians in their letter had put a question to Paul. Such cases must be put aside in the letters to Timothy.

This consideration perhaps explains what seems to the present writer to be the most disappointing feature of the Pastoral Epistles. Although the dangers of the free competition in teaching by unauthorized and often badly qualified teachers (the so-called "false teachers") is in Paul's mind throughout the three epistles as the greatest danger to his Asian churches, yet he simply denounces these volunteer teachers without suggesting a remedy. The only permanent remedy lay in the creation of a system of Christian teaching on a sufficiently high level. Such a system would have kept the higher education in Christian hands, whereas the absence of it had the result described by the late Dr. Bigg in *The Church's Task in the Roman Empire*, namely, that the education of Christian children lay largely in the hands of pagan teachers. I do not think that Paul would have acquiesced in the incapacity of the church to solve this great problem. His fertile mind and organizing ability might have organized the means to this end if he had lived longer; but at this time he only points out the actual danger and suggests no means whereby it may be overcome. Probably he had no such object in view for the moment. He was thinking of nothing else except putting Timothy on his guard, urging him to "take heed to the *diakonia*" which he had received. Only in 2 Timothy 2:2 is there perhaps an obscure reference to the beginning of a remedy for the evil: 'the things which you have heard from me among many witnesses, the same commit you to faithful men, who shall be able to teach others also." This does not refer to *paradosis*, the transmission to successors, but to the actual choosing of suitable teachers under Timothy.[3] Probably, however, only "clerical" teaching is implied (see chapter 8 on this subject).

Hence in 1 Timothy, Paul simply reiterates the sound doctrine and denounces the unsound. If the germ and principle of growth is sound, the rest will come. The Spirit will guide the healthy church in the constructive program which lies before it. We may at first feel disappointed that no advice is given regarding the right education which is needed to replace the false education; but Paul did not regard this as the important matter to urge at that moment on Timothy. "Keep the seed sound" is his theme. For the individual the fundamental fact, the sound germ, is "have faith"; for the teacher it is "hold the sound doctrine."

This does not mean that there is not a great deal to be added. Faith is only the germ, sound doctrine is the germ; but the germ, if healthy and strong, will grow up into the perfect life and the perfect church without any help from Paul. The germ brings with it the Spirit of God: it is the Spirit of God. The individual who has faith will work out his own salvation. The church in which the sound doctrine is taught will grow on the right lines of development. That is after all the fundamental doctrine of Paulinism.

On the other hand Paul also uses the terms *diakonos* and *diakonia* in a wider and more general sense to indicate the service or the ministration rendered by one who carries into effect the desire of another or gives help or good to another person or persons. So in Romans 15:31, "that my *diakonia* to Jerusalem may be acceptable to the saints"; 1 Corinthians 12:5, "there are diverse kinds of *diakoniai*"; 2 Corinthians 3:7–9, "the *diakonia* of death . . . of the Spirit . . . of judgment . . . of righteousness"; 2 Corinthians 5:18, "the *diakonia* of reconciliation." In all these and other cases the *diakonos* supplies or arranges something at the order and will of another, even though he may appear to be in authority, as was the case with Paul in the *diakonia* to Jerusalem (Rom 15:31), or Barnabas and Saul in the older *diakonia* to Jerusalem (Acts 12:25), in both of which the object is to carry and distribute charity to the poor.

31

Supremacy of the Family Tie in the Pastorals: Is This a Pauline Doctrine?

Owing to the compressed character of Paul's writing, and the way in which he trusts to his correspondents to appreciate his point of view and to understand and take for granted much that he does not explicitly state, it is frequently the case that a quite indispensable preliminary to the proper comprehension of some passage in his writings is to make oneself clear about what he omits to say and assumes as already familiar to his reader or readers. Especially is this the case with such a complex subject as the constitution of society within the Christian congregation, the family relationship and obligation, and the relation of the congregational unity to the family and to the individual. That this vast subject should be exhaustively discussed within the narrow limits of the short first letter to Timothy, even if the letter were specially devoted to it, is obviously impossible. But when the subject is only alluded to on account of its bearing on other things, this indirect treatment must inevitably be incomplete, and must assume that Paul's general attitude towards the whole subject is well known to Timothy.

This consideration must be weighed in discussing whether and how far the treatment of marriage in the Pastoral Epistles implies a different point of view from that which Paul occupied when writing his first letter to the Corinthians. Assuming that the Pastoral Epistles were written by Paul to his coadjutors Timothy and Titus, who were both familiar with the conditions in the Corinthian church, we may say at once that he could and would count on their knowledge of his earlier views about this subject. Both had been engaged actively in the work at Corinth. Timothy had been associated with Paul in the second letter to the Corinthians. Titus had been sent on a special mission to Corinth during a critical condition of affairs in that congregation.

Further, surely it is equally obvious that both Timothy and Titus must have been offended by any serious inconsistency between Paul's former views about marriage and those expressed in the Pastorals. It is, therefore, unquestionable that either there is no real and grave inconsistency between 1 Corinthians and the Pastorals, nothing beyond a certain enlargement or modification of the outlook towards which Paul had been moving in the intervening years and for which his readers were prepared, or the authorship is open to suspicion.

Any seeming discrepancy is, as I believe, fully explicable as perfectly natural in the circumstances, through two considerations: (1) Paul counted on Timothy and Titus to understand much that is not expressly stated in the letters addressed to them; and (2) Paul was writing to people in practical charge of congregations, and therefore he confined himself for the most part to the statement of general principles, and left the treatment of exceptional cases to the judgment of the administrator under the guidance of the Holy Spirit.

(1) One cannot doubt, as I think, that Paul to the last hour of his life believed and knew with the whole power of his nature that some persons were, like himself, right in avoiding marriage and devoting themselves exclusively to the higher life. One also feels that Timothy and Titus were aware of Paul's views on this matter; and it seems probable that Timothy at least acted on them. He was carried off to the work of a wandering missionary at a very early age, and was probably absorbed wholly in this engrossing kind of occupation. One feels that Paul would have been disappointed if Timothy had declined from this course of life into love for a woman, or into marriage as a mere family duty. If this full understanding on the part of all three is presupposed, I see no real inconsistency between 1 Corinthians and the Pastorals; and this presupposition is easy and natural. Timothy and Titus knew perfectly all that Paul said in 1 Corinthians 7 and had doubtless often repeated on other occasions.

(2) The family unity is the strongest factor in the unity of the congregation. Such is the fundamental idea in the Pastorals; and such is the practical fact of social life. This has to be emphasized to the administrators of Asia and Crete. That some cases of celibacy would occur in their congregations needed no notice; they were aware of this. What needed emphasis was that, when the family relationship existed, it entails duties which must be discharged and

from which there can hardly be any exemption. Hence the strong language of 1 Timothy 5:8: "If any provides not for his own who are most closely connected with him, he has denied the faith, and is worse than an unbeliever." The Authorized and the Revised Versions seem to misrepresent τῶν ἰδίων καὶ μάλιστα οἰκείων. By the renderings "for his own and specially for those of his own house" (or "his own household"), two classes are apparently specified; but the omission of the article before μάλιστα shows that ἰδίων and μάλιστα οἰκωείων both describe one single class, "those who are his own and specially closely connected with him."

This principle should be taken in the universal sense. Parents and grandparents are ἴδιοι and οἰκεῖοι to a child; children are ἴδιοι and οἰκεῖοι to a parent or grandparent. The parent cannot escape his duty to a child, nor the child to a parent or grandparent. So with other family relations in their order of closeness.

Further, what if there is imminent a collision between this rule and the rule of 1 Corinthians 7:5–8? What if the father of a household desires to devote himself to the divine life? Is he free to do so? May he argue that, as family cares take up too much of his time and attention, he may shake them off and give his undivided mind to work for the glory of God and the good of the church? May he conclude that for him, with his special talents and aspirations and character, marriage was a mistake and the care of a family only a hindrance to a higher range of activity, from which he ought to free himself? So also in the case of a child. Can he free himself from duty to parents?

That was a question which Paul had not answered in 1 Corinthians, because it was a question that was not consciously present to him then.[1] He was guarding the freedom of individual choice against the universal rule of marriage, which the Corinthians were proposing as a wise measure, and which Paul could never allow.[2]

In the Pastorals, however, it was inevitable that this question should emerge. It is a question which must often be thrust on the notice of one who is charged with the care of a congregation. Ought one to be free to consecrate oneself to the divine life, and thereby become free from responsibility for his family? Paul now answers most emphatically "No!" in 1 Timothy 5:8.

I cannot agree with those who take 1 Timothy 5:8 in relation only with 1 Timothy 5:4, and regard it as prescribing a rule only for children in relation to their parents. It prescribes a universal principle, which lies at the basis of church life and of healthy society.

As to the question alluded to above, whether there had occurred any enlargement or modification of Paul's views during the years that he intervened between the writing of 1 Corinthians and the Pastoral Epistles, I cordially agree with the opinion stated by Principal Garvie[3] that no development can be traced in the apostle's teaching during the period in which it is known to us. That a great and vast development occurred at some time in his thought is, of course, certain. He had to rethink his whole view of life and God during the early years of his career as a Christian. He had to grow from the Hebrew-Pharisaic outlook to the Pauline-Christian outlook. That needed much time and meditation, and required an almost complete remaking of his mind. But the process was practically completed before his mission to the Gentiles began in Acts 13:2. There is no essential difference between the gospel of Paul in Thessalonians and in Ephesians and in Timothy. The differences which undoubtedly do exist between those epistles are in part due to the varying character and position and power of comprehension among the recipients. The needs and the powers of a set of pagans who had had only a very few weeks of teaching were very different from those of a congregation that had behind it years of experience and thought. Those pagan converts of Paul had to be raised first to the much higher level of Hebrew thought and moral view and thereafter to the level of the Christian mind.

Moreover, while there was no development in the essential character of Paul's gospel, there was a development in his plans and in his method and power of presenting his gospel to the Greco-Roman world. He learned by experience how to use the opportunities of that world, and how to turn all the instruments of civilization to serve his purposes. We know that he made tentative plans and abandoned his first plans in the prosecution of his work. The roads on which he first entered he soon abandoned for new and more important paths; and he finally made the great central highway of the empire through Ephesus and Corinth the theater of his main effort.

Perhaps also there was some development in his power of expressing his gospel in a way that should be intelligible and convincing to his converts, morally undeveloped as they were. He knew their hearts and thoughts from his childhood in Tarsus; but even so the task was no easy one. That his presentation of his thought was modified through experience is evident from a comparison between 1 Thessalonians and 2 Timothy. As has been stated in chapter 28, he is in both those letters much occupied with the thought of death and the last things; but how differently does he express himself in the second letter! He had learned that the expression used in the earlier was open to misconception and therefore unsuited for his purpose.

Gradually he learned to fulfill his task better, namely, to interpret the wisdom of God, to explain Christ who is the wisdom of God (1 Cor. 1:24, 30), not merely to destroy the false sham wisdom, but to build up the true wisdom, to be the wise master builder who lays the foundation on which others may complete the superstructure. Such is the development of Paul, the adequate expression of Christian higher thought for the first time in the Greek tongue, and not in a technical jargon nor in a barbarous Hebraicizing kind of Greek, but in the natural familiar language of the Greek-speaking races.

Chapter Notes

Introduction

1. Edwin Yamauchi, "Ramsay's Views on Archaeology in Asia Minor Reviewed" in *The New Testament Student and His World,* ed. John H. Skilton (Phillipsburg, N.J.: Presbyterian & Reformed, 1982), 27.

Chapter One

1. Many prefer to take the view that, because the Pastoral Epistles approximate markedly to the point of view and standard of thought which are found in the Acts, therefore the Epistles must have been written at the same time as the book of the Acts was finally composed. Especially those who regarded the Acts as a second-century book must necessarily take this view. The present writer's reasons are elaborated on pages 20–25 and have partly been stated in *The Expositor*, February–May, 1909.

Chapter Three

1. It is a curious example of pedantry that the word for "tarry" (προσμεῖναι) is reckoned by some among the words peculiar to the Pastorals and therefore un-Pauline. The sense of verbal propriety is defective in a scholar who finds any difficulty in understanding that any writer may occasionally, or even only once, use some compound of a Greek verb, which he often employs in the simple form. Moreover, the word occurs about Paul in Acts 18:18.

Chapter Four

1. It would doubtless be better to speak of "congregations" in the plural. As being in charge for Paul at Ephesus, Timothy was to exercise surveillance over all the congregations and churches of the province Asia. Ephesus was the central point and heart of the whole church organization of the province.
2. See, e.g., *Luke the Physician* (London: Hodder & Stoughton, 1908), 253ff.
3. This passage in the *Agamemnon* is more genealogical in Paley's text than in that of the manuscripts or of later editors, but the idea is there in all forms of the text.

Chapter Five

1. (London: Hodder & Stoughton, 1907), 425–30.
2. Of course abbreviating, but never misrepresenting, the speeches.
3. This point is briefly noticed in the first chapter of *Luke the Physician*, 25.
4. Incidentally, it deserves notice that this scheme (Rom. 15:28) furnishes a clear proof that Paul knew Latin, and intended to address himself to the people of the Spanish cities in Latin. He could not be dreaming of addressing them in Greek, but Latin was sufficient for his purposes. Spain was thoroughly Latinized, and the Spanish cities were all raised to the Latin rank a few years later by Vespasian. Greek was never known by the people except in a few Greek colonies on the east coast of Spain; and it is doubtful whether even in them it was used as late as A.D. 57. That Paul spoke Latin is argued in *St. Paul the Traveller*, 225.

Chapter Six

1. I think it is necessary to understand that the principle of election was instituted. The word χειροτονήσαντες in 14:23 might not be sufficient to prove this, taken alone; but in conjunction with subsequent custom and with Paul's allusions to aiming at office and with Greek habits it must be read in this way.
2. Some difficulty has been felt as to the way of reconciling the narrative in the Acts with the allusions which Paul makes in his letter to the movements of Timothy. According to the former, Paul was convoyed from Berea to the seacoast by some of the brethren. At the coast some change occurred in his plans; and the brethren brought him to Athens, and returned to Berea carrying a message to Silas and Timothy to come to Paul with all speed. The residence in Athens was evidently cut short, and it was in Corinth that Silas and Timothy rejoined Paul. Luke says nothing about Timothy's mission to Thessalonica; and if we had only the Acts to go by, we should understand that Timothy with Silas returned from Berea to join Paul and, finding in Athens that he had gone to Corinth, followed him there. But from Paul himself we gather that he sent directions from Athens to Timothy to go to Thessalonica, and that the latter came from Thessalonica to rejoin him. There seems to be no inconsistency between the two. The one adds to the other, but does not disagree with it. Paul sent from Athens to Timothy and Silas, bidding them come to him there with all speed; to this we must add that they were to use all speed in finishing up their work. That they had some work in hand may be regarded as certain: Paul and his subordinates were always busy. That they had separate pieces of work in hand is shown by the whole situation. There were two pieces of work to do: Paul himself was prevented from doing them. The inference is that Timothy was to come to Athens through Thessalonica, confirming the church there and appointing officials, while Silas was to finish up the work at Berea and then come on to Athens. Finally both came to him in Corinth "from Macedonia." If they had both come from Berea, Luke would naturally have said "from Berea."
3. So Hellenic cities in Asia Minor generally contained assemblies or societies of the *neoi* or men and the *presbyteroi* or elders.

4. In 1 Thessalonians 5:12 and 14 the same word νουθετέω is applied to the duty of the ordinary members and of the προιστάμενοι in the congregation.
5. Acts 1:17; 6:4.
6. See the preceding chapter.
7. 1 Timothy 2:12 states that a woman must not teach or hold authority.
8. Presbyter is the term used in 1 Timothy 5:17–20 and Titus 1:5–9 to indicate the bishop of 3:1–7.

Chapter Seven

1. ἐπαγγέλλεσθαι regularly implies that the persons mentioned came before the public with promises in order to gain supporters. It is applied to candidates for municipal favor and votes in the Greek cities, who publicly announced what they intended to do for the general benefit, if they gained popular support. The word used in Titus 1:16, "they profess that they know God," is ὁμολογοῦσιν, which carries no such connotation and should rather be rendered "they confess" or "acknowledge" that God has been duly and properly set before them, and have not the excuse of ignorance, but their actions show revolt from him.

Chapter Eight

1. Especially 1 Timothy 1:4–10, 19–20; 4:1–8; 6:3–5, 9, 20–21; 2 Timothy 2:14–18, 23–25; 3:6–8; 4:4; Titus 1:9–11, 13–16, 2:1–3:9. Some of these refer to the future and are expressed in the future tense, but they refer not to future dangers and heresies, but to the inevitable consequences of present errors.
2. I would venture to correct in this respect Professor Deissmann's teaching in his valuable articles in *The Expositor* (February–April 1909).
3. It was only after the preceding pages had been written, when I began to put on paper in order the features of the Ephesian teachers, that the analogy with Juvenal's description occurred to my mind with startling vividness.
4. Wizards would be nearer the meaning of γόητες than "impostors," but the two ideas pass into one another.
5. This passage relates to the future, but the future is the effect of the teaching that has already begun.
6. It has sometimes been wrongly inferred from 3.83 that Juvenal is here describing Greek slaves who have risen in the world through the Roman slave market. But the line will not bear this inference; and the picture as a whole is that of free Greek strangers, who win their way first as teachers, and afterwards by their universal talents and their versatility.
7. In Ephesus "from the fifth to the tenth hour" (Acts 19:9 Bezan text): he evidently worked as a craftsman from the break of day to the fifth hour (20:34).
8. One need hardly guard against the misinterpretation that this is Paul's characterization of all women. The master of Luke did not think like that, but he was painfully well aware that such is one class of women.
9. *The Letters to the Seven Churches,* ed. Mark W. Wilson (Peabody, Mass.: Hendrickson, 1994), 174.
10. Some evidence bearing on this matter is collected in "The Church of

Lycaonia in the Fourth Century" in *Luke the Physician, and other Studies in the History of Religion* (London: Hodder and Stoughton, 1908), 330–410.

11. *The Church's Task under the Roman Empire* (Oxford: Clarendon, 1905), 25–26.

Chapter Nine

1. I cannot feel any doubt that this is the right interpretation. There was no real intention to hear the argument again; postponement, when a preacher is speaking by invitation and has not yet finished his discourse, is equivalent to condemnation.

2. In *The Apocryphal New Testament* edited by J. K. Elliott (Oxford: Clarendon, 1993), 366–67.

3. "Life subject apparently to death, yet never dying, but reproducing itself in new forms, different and yet the same. This self-identity under varying forms, this annihilation of death through the power of self-reproduction was the object of the enthusiastic worship of Asia Minor with all its self-abandonment. . . The parent is the child, the mother is the daughter, the father the son; they seem to men different; religion teaches that they are the same, that death and birth are only two aspects of one idea, and that the birth is only the completion of the incomplete apparent death" (*Luke the Physician*, 205).

4. See a series of papers in the *Expository Times* (October 1898–January 1899); also the *Expositor* (March 1900), 212.

5. No mention is made in 1 Timothy 1:20 of the church or of Jesus as associating themselves with the action of Paul, but the fact that Paul mentions only his own action constitutes no proof that the others were not cooperating with him. It may be assumed as a matter of course that σὺν τῇ δυνάμει τοῦ κυρίου ἡμῶν Ἰησοῦ was as true in the one case as in the other; and if Paul passes in silence over the cooperation of Jesus, it is quite possible that the church also is omitted. The facts were familiar to Timothy.

6. This does not, it need hardly be said, imply that every episode and verse in the New Testament is equally certain and authoritative. Variations in degree of authoritative character occur. Some episodes do not rest on such good testimony as others. The Gospels are not free from traces of the age when they were written, though these are few. To distinguish these later elements is the function of a sane and unprejudiced criticism, which as yet has not been consistently applied.

7. In 1 Timothy 1:20 the association with Hymenaeus is in itself sufficiently distinctive.

Chapter Eleven

1. The meaning of this enigmatic passage in 2 Thessalonians is more fully discussed in *The Cities of St. Paul*, 425–29.

Chapter Twelve

1. On the strict custom as to complete veiling of women which prevailed at Tarsus—a custom previously unknown to but highly approved by Dion Chrysostom (when he visited Tarsus about A.D. 112): he had been accustomed to Hellenic cities where women were not

veiled, though they were treated as distinctly inferior creatures—see *The Cities of St. Paul*, 202.

2. *Historical Commentary on Galatians* (London: Hodder and Stoughton, 1899), 386.
3. *Letters to the Seven Churches*, 118. The circumstance that Ignatius was accustomed to silent prayer in the assembly would have to be taken account of in that chapter from which I am quoting.
4. I mean a model to be imitated, not a form of words to be slavishly repeated. But as soon as the custom begins that the whole congregation should speak any prayer aloud, there must be a set form; otherwise there is confusion and anarchy.
5. I am deeply indebted to the Rev. G. H. Box for an admirably instructive statement on this subject and on the relation of 1 Timothy 2:8 to Jewish ritual, which I should have liked to print entire as it stands if I had his permission. Dr. Sanday kindly procured the statement for me; and favored me with some notes of his own impressions, which I have used in the text. My own views were written and sent to the printer before receiving the statement, but it does not necessitate any change in them, and I have left them as they were formed. The last five paragraphs have the advantage of being written subsequently.
6. In the ritual of Ben Tyrannos, for example, complete ablution is prescribed for the impure before entering the temple. Foucart (*Associations Religieuses*, 219) is, however, surely in error when he understands κατακέφαλα λούσασθαι as *se jeter de l'eau sur la tête*. It must denote complete washing from the head downwards.
7. See *The Expositor* (October 1908), 299 and (November 1908), 407.
8. *Cities and Bishoprics of Phrygia* (Oxford: Clarendon Press, 1895–1897), 2.545ff., 674ff.; *St. Paul the Traveller*, 141–44.

Chapter Thirteen

1. Although that is not stated expressly here, it is in Paul's mind always (1 Cor. 14:34–35; Titus 2:5).
2. The thought is universal; and though the expression begins in the generic singular "she," it changes ungrammatically to the plural "if they continue."
3. *St. Paul the Traveller*, 354; *The Cities of St. Paul*, 216ff.
4. I give my own idea of this much-disputed metaphysical term, which perhaps nobody will accept as a translation. But at least all recognize that the idea in Aristotle's mind was highly abstract and metaphysical, and that the words are chosen from the commonest range of expression used by every Greek peasant.
5. I have been trying in vain to recall the writer and the book. My memory in a vague way connects the incident with George Eliot.
6. The context removes all doubt: the following words are enough—

δεινὸν τὸ τίκτειν ἐστίν· οὐδὲ γὰρ κακῶς
πάσχοντι μῖσος ὧν τέκῃ προσγίγνεται

which the late Professor Lewis Campbell renders—

To be a mother hath a marvellous power,
No injury can make one hate one's child.

Moreover, the translation which is condemned in the text above approaches perilously near the grammatical crime of taking the present infinitive in the sense of the aorist infinitive.

7. With this compare 1 Timothy 5:1, 2: παρακάλει ... πρεσβυτέρας ὡς μητέρας.
8. The writer has studied this side of Horace's poetry in *Macmillan's Magazine* (October 1897), 450–57, on "The Childhood of Horace," and advanced a theory to account for it.
9. Unknown also elsewhere in the New Testament.

Chapter Fourteen

1. The obscure and difficult adjective καλός, one of the first that a beginner in the Greek language learns to translate, and one of the most difficult for an advanced scholar to understand, unites the ideas of good and honorable and beautiful in a thoroughly Greek fashion.
2. Meyer-Weiss in *Kritisch-exegetischer Kommentar* refuse to accept any such implication in ἔργου, but I cannot think that their view is justifiable.
3. *Church in the Roman Empire*, 288, 368; *Luke the Physician*, 154, 353–54; *Pauline and Other Studies*, 118, 382–86, 402–3.
4. For the text of this epitaph see *Cities and Bishoprics of Phrygia*, 2.722–29; cf. J. B. Lightfoot, *The Apostolic Fathers* (Peabody, Mass.: Hendrickson, [1889–90] 1989), 2.1.492–501.
5. *Pauline and Other Studies*, 384–85.
6. Compare the examples given in chapter 3 and in the preceding chapter.
7. That the word πάροινος must be taken in its own sense, and not as a figure of speech implying only "brawler," seems beyond question; see Meyer-Weiss in *Kritisch-exegetischer Kommentar*. So also πλήκτης must be interpreted literally.
8. That was one of the wearing anxieties in "the care of all the churches" (2 Cor. 11:28), which were always with him.
9. It is, of course, indirectly implied in ἀνεπίλημπτος (1 Tim. 3:2) and ἀνέγκλητος (Titus 1:6, 7; cf. 1 Tim. 3:10), but good reputation among the brethren is not formally mentioned as a condition.

Chapter Fifteen

1. μὴ πάροινον with its results and ἀφιλάργον. One cannot draw much distinction between those epithets and the different epithets applied to the deacons. Instead of ἀφιλάργος, αἰσχροκερδεῖς is said of the deacons in 1 Timothy and of the bishops in Titus. The phrase about wine-drinking is a little more emphatic in the case of deacons, μὴ οἴνῳ πολλῷ προσέχοντας. On the sense of the other pair of epithets, see the next chapter.
2. δοκιμαζέσθωσαν.
3. Dass eine solche Prüfung hinsichtlich der Bischöfe angestellt würde versteht sich allerdings von selbst. (That such a test employed concerning the bishops was certainly self-explanatory.)
4. Even if there was not a probation in the sense of making the person under consideration do the work of the office on trial for some time,

there was at least a probation in the sense of some much more rigor-
ous and practical trial than was imposed on one who was being considered as a possible bishop.

5. In the preceding chapter it was an omission not to lay stress on this
aspect of the matter: what is there said is, I think, true in itself, but
not complete.

Chapter Sixteen

1. See *Luke the Physician*, 393–95.

Chapter Seventeen

1. Alfred Plummer, "The Pastoral Epistles" in *The Expositor's Bible* (New
York, 1888), 111: "Three things come out very clearly from this passage, confirming what has been found in the New Testament. (1) There
is a clear distinction made between clergy and laity. (2) This distinction is not a temporary arrangement, but is the basis of a permanent
organization. (3) A person who has been duly promoted to the ranks of
the clergy as a presbyter or bishop holds that position for life. Unless
he is guilty of some serious offense, to depose him is no light sin."

Chapter Nineteen

1. Visions like those described in the two passages quoted may be taken
generally (not always) as the expression and confirmation of thoughts
that were floating in the mind of the seer.
2. See especially chapter 14; also chapters 15–17.
3. ἐν τάχει and βραδύνω.
4. There are always certain to be many points of close resemblance
between different adumbrations of the "good man," sketched in the
same society by various members of it, even from totally different
points of view.
5. That at least one of Luke's and Matthew's authorities and a first sketch
of Mark were composed by that time seems to me beyond question.
6. From the grammatical point of view, the tense (aorist) needs notice
in this case. The aorist is right because the entire life is expressed as
a statement of historical fact. There is no reference to a series of
appearances of angels to see, as angels come to visit people when
sent to do so: "He was seen by angels."

Chapter Twenty

1. Simon Magus at Samaria, as described by Luke (Acts 8:9ff.), may be
taken as a typical example of the false teacher who is within the
church and most dangerous to it.
2. It is not Paul's purpose to specify the nature and scope of the prohibition. He may probably have included more than one school of teaching about foods, for example, perhaps (1) Jewish distinction of clean
and unclean foods, as such, and (2) prohibition of eating all flesh
(which was a common teaching in certain Oriental lands).

Chapter Twenty-Two

1. In the translation "man of one woman," the sacredness of the family tie
is emphasized equally strongly, though from a different point of view.

2. Hence the Christian was called οἰκέτης θεοῦ in Lycaonia; this phrase implies that the church was the οἶκος θεοῦ (see *Luke the Physician and other Studies*, 408).
3. οἰκοδεσποτειν. In an unpublished inscription of Derbe, which I copied in 1901, a woman is called ἡ καλὴ οἰκοδεσποτίς. This is probably an allusion to the phrase of 1 Timothy. The word is not elsewhere used by Paul; but that is natural since the importance of the family in the Christian life never forms a topic in any of the earlier letters.
4. Taking this idea in the wide sense described in chapter 13, which includes as part of its scope the narrower and more literal sense of the term.
5. In this place I can only assume what is said in chapters 25 and 26 of my *Historical Commentary on First Corinthians*.
6. "Neither Jew *nor* Greek, neither bond *nor* free, no male *and* female." In section 40 of my *Historical Commentary on Galatians*, the bearing of this verse is treated at length.
7. 1 Corinthians 11:39; Ephesians 5:23, 33; 1 Timothy 2:11.
8. There is opportunity in the lists of vices in other letters to introduce words of this class; but the vocabulary of vituperation is rich.

Chapter Twenty-Three

1. I do not mean, of course, that this is absent from the earlier epistles, but it is not emphasized so strongly, though it is apparent in them, for example, in Ephesians.
2. Such seems to be the meaning of 13:3; see *St. Paul the Traveller*, 65.
3. *Ecclesia*, 184.

Chapter Twenty-Four

1. There are some examples of an intermediate class of ἄνδρες between the *neoi* and the *gerontes*; but this is rare and exceptional. Generally, we find the double, not the triple classification of the full-grown men. On this subject many authorities have written: references may be found in *Cities and Bishoprics of Phrygia*, 1.110ff.
2. For example, at Chios the *epheboi* are divided into three classes—νεώτεροι, μέσοι, and πρεσβύτεροι (*Corpus Inscriptionum Graecarum* [CIG] 2214).
3. The translation "command" in the RV (and NIV) is too strong: παραγγέλλω is rather to "announce," to "charge," than to "command" (cf. 1 Tim. 1:5, τὸ δὲ τέλος τῆς παραγγελίας ἐστὶν ἀγάπη; compare also 1:3, 5:7, 6:17 where the same verb is suited to Timothy). But in the case of Titus 3:3 ἐπιταγη, (a much stronger term as in 1 Tim. 1:1) is used, never παραγγέλλω or παραγγελία
4. 1 Timothy 5:20: "them that sin reprove in the sight of all."

Chapter Twenty-Five

1. *Luke the Physician*, 304.

Chapter Twenty-Six

1. This second period, from twenty to forty years of age, corresponds roughly to the Greek conception of youth, νεότης, as has been shown in a previous section. So in Latin *juvenis* often means a man of military age.

2. I take this from Rudyard Kipling's story "The Miracle of Purun Bhagat" in the *Second Jungle Book*, a story which appears to me to be the finest piece of oriental work that he has done.
3. *The Expositor* (December 1908), 547–48.
4. *The Expositor* (November 1908), 385–419.

Chapter Twenty-Eight

1. The punctuation which (with various good authorities) I adopt seems preferable to that of the Revisers, who take the following rhythmical words as the "faithful saying." The other places where a "faithful saying" occurs favor this: compare especially 1 Timothy 4:8–10, also Titus 3:8. In 1 Timothy 1:15 the "faithful saying" follows these words, but in that case it is expressed with accusative and infinitive (so also in 1 Timothy 3:1).

Chapter Twenty-Nine

1. Translated from Steffen in *Zeitschrift Neutestamentliche Wissenschraft* (1901), 2.124, by Dr. Kennedy in *St. Paul's Conception of the Last Things*, 6.
2. See two papers in *The Expositor* (June, July, 1907) by the present writer.

Chapter Thirty

1. Compare 1 Corinthians 3:5: Paul and Apollos are *diakonoi*; 2 Corinthians 6:4: "*diakonoi* of God"; and 2 Corinthians 3:6: "God made us sufficient as *diakonoi* of a new covenant" (Paul and Timothy or Paul alone); 2 Corinthians 15:23, Ephesians 3:7.
2. On Colossians 4:17 see the remarks in a subsequent paragraph.
3. The verb is παρατίθεσθαι not παραδιδόναι.

Chapter Thirty-One

1. It is not explicitly stated or directly answered; but indirectly and implicitly it is answered in 1 Corinthians 7:2, exactly as in the Pastorals.
2. See my *Historical Commentary on First Corinthians*, chapter 22 (improved in chapter 25). I am not convinced by my friend Professor John Massie's diverse opinion as to the nature of the Corinthians' suggestion.
3. *The Expositor* (February 1911), 180ff.